JORGE LUIS BORGES

JORGE LUIS BORGES
THE LAST INTERVIEW
and OTHER CONVERSATIONS

MELVILLE HOUSE
BROOKLYN · LONDON

JORGE LUIS BORGES: THE LAST INTERVIEW

Copyright © 2013 by Melville House Publishing

"Original Mythology" © 1968 by Richard Burgin. First published in
Conversations with Jorge Luis Borges. The interview was conducted in English.

"Borges and I" © 1980 by *Artful Dodge.* Reprinted by permission.
The interview was conducted in English.

"The Last Interview" was originally broadcast on La Isla FM Radio, 1985.
© 1985, 2013 by María Kodama and Gloria López Lecube, used by permission
of the Wylie Agency LLC and Gloria López Lecube. Translation from the Spanish
of the "Last Interview" © 2013 by Kit Maude.

First Melville House printing: June 2013

Melville House Publishing   8 Blackstock Mews
145 Plymouth Street   and   Islington
Brooklyn, NY 11201   London N4 2BT

mhpbooks.com   facebook.com/mhpbooks   @melvillehouse

ISBN: 978-1-61219-204-8

Manufactured in the United States of America
1 3 5 7 9 10 8 6 4 2

A catalog record for this book is available
from the Library of Congress.

CONTENTS

ORIGINAL MYTHOLOGY

INTERVIEWS BY RICHARD BURGIN

FROM *CONVERSATIONS WITH JORGE LUIS BORGES*, 1968

One of the many pleasures the stars (in which I don't believe) have granted me is in literary and metaphysical dialogue. Since both these designations run the risk of seeming a bit pretentious, I should clarify that dialogue for me is not a form of polemics, of monologue or magisterial dogmatism, but of shared investigation. I can't refer to dialogue without thinking of my father, of Rafael Cansinos-Asséns, of Macedonio Fernández, and of many others I can't begin to mention— since the most notable names on any list will always turn out to be those omitted. In spite of my impersonal concept of dialogue, my questioners tell me (and my memory confirms) that I tend to become a bit of a missionary and to preach, not without a certain monotony, the virtues of Old English and Old Norse, of Schopenhauer and Berkeley, of Emerson and Frost. The readers of this volume will realize that. It is enough for me to say that if I am rich in anything, it is in perplexities rather than in certainties. A colleague declares from his chair that philosophy is clear and precise understanding; I would define it as that organization of the essential perplexities of man.

I have many pleasant memories of the United States, especially of Texas and New England. In Cambridge, Massachusetts, I spent many hours in leisurely conversation with Richard Burgin. It seemed to me he had no particular axe to grind; there was no imposition in his questioning or even a demand for a reply. There was nothing didactic either. There was a sense of timelessness.

Rereading these pages, I think I have expressed myself, in fact confessed myself, better than in those I have written in solitude with excess care and vigilance. The exchange of thoughts is a condition necessary for all love, all friendship and all real dialogue. Two men who can speak together can enrich and broaden themselves indefinitely. What comes forth from me does not surprise me as much as what I receive from the other.

I know there are people in the world who have the curious desire to know me better. For some seventy years, without too much effort, I have been working towards the same end. Walt Whitman has already said it:

"I think I know little or nothing of my real life."

Richard Burgin has helped me to know myself.

—Jorge Luis Borges

On the day I found out that Jorge Luis Borges was coming to America, to Cambridge, I ran from Harvard Square to my room in Central Square, over a mile away, in no more than five minutes. The rest of that summer of 1967 seemed only a preparation for his arrival. Everywhere I went I spoke of Borges.

When it was time for school again and I returned to Brandeis for my last year as an undergraduate, I met a very pretty girl from Brazil named Flo Bildner who seemed even more enthusiastic about Borges than I was. Whenever we'd run into each other, we'd talk for three or four hours at a stretch about Borges. After one such conversation, we decided we had to meet him.

I remember the schemes we proposed, elaborate, involuted, outrageous schemes, more complicated than a Russian novel. Finally we rejected all of them. There was only one thing to do; Flo had his telephone number, she should call him up and say we wanted to see him. Strangely, miraculously, the plan worked.

It was November 21, it was grey outside and raining slightly, it was two days before Thanksgiving. Our meeting was set for 6:30, so Flo and I split up in the afternoon, each to go out and buy him a present. Of course, there is something futile about buying a gift for Borges. He simply has no need or desire for any symbol of gratitude for his company. He always makes you feel that it is he who is the grateful one, and that your company is the only gift he needs. In any event, after wandering up and down the long streets of Boston, going through department stores, book stores, and record stores, I finally bought him a record of Bach's Fourth and Fifth Brandenburg concertos on which my father played violin. Back in Cambridge, I met Flo holding her gift, four long-stemmed yellow roses.

The distance from Harvard Square to Borges's apartment on Concord Avenue was only some four or five blocks, yet to us it seemed almost as great an odyssey as the voyage of Ulysses. I think I have forgotten nothing or almost nothing of that evening. I remember the calm in the air after the rain; Flo's eyes as wide and green as tropical limes; the mirrors in the Continental Hotel, where we stopped to perfect our appearance; the thousands of wet leaves on the footpaths. I remember stopping at the wrong address, ringing the doorbell, then apologizing hastily when a young woman answered who had never heard of Borges. I remember how we turned away and ran almost a block laughing—a dreamlike kind of laughter of dizziness, anxiety and an intoxicating kind of happiness.

Then through the glass of a door we saw him, holding a cane and being helped to a lift by a man with crutches. We ran into the building, introduced ourselves, and helped both of them into the lift. The other man, in his early thirties perhaps and a physicist from MIT, was helping Borges in his study of Persian literature. Borges was dressed in a conservative but elegant grey suit with a pale blue necktie. The small apartment he shared with his wife seemed peculiarly empty. There were some ten or fifteen books on his bookshelf, a twelve-inch TV in the living room and a few magazines on a table. He seemed nervous or ill at ease at first, particularly when we gave him our presents. His wife was out with some friends, so Flo happily assumed the role of woman of the house. She went to the kitchen to fill a vase with water for the roses.

"Don't worry where you sit," he said to me. "I can't see anything." I went to sit down on a couch, but Borges was up again in a start. "Do you want anything to drink? Wine, Scotch, or water?" I declined, but Flo decided to fix everybody a drink. Borges was back in front of me again. "Did you come just to chat or did you have something special to ask me?" If I had known a day or a week before that he would ask this question I wouldn't have known what to say. Now the words came out of their own accord.

"I'm going to write a book about you and I thought I might ask you some questions."

And so we began to talk. Within fifteen minutes we were talking about Faulkner, Whitman, Melville, Kafka, Henry James, Dostoevsky and Schopenhauer. Every five minutes or so he would interrupt the flow of his conversation by saying, "Am I boring you? Am I disappointing you?" Then he said something that moved me very deeply. "I am nearly seventy and I could disguise myself as a young man, but then I would not be myself and you would see through it."

He is, perhaps above all other things, honest—so honest that your first reaction is to doubt him. But as I was to find out, he means everything he says, and when he is joking, somehow he makes sure you know it. Towards the end of our conversation he made some remarks about time. "After two or three chapters of *The Trial* you know he will never be judged, you see through the method. It's the same thing in *The Castle*, which is more or less unreadable. I imitated Kafka once, but next time I hope to imitate a better writer. Sometimes great writers are not recognized. Who knows, there may be a young man or an old man writing now who *is* great. I should say a writer should have another lifetime to see if he's appreciated." Later he would say to me: "... I have uttered the wish that if I am born again I will have no personal memories of my other life. I mean to say, I don't want to go on being Jorge Luis Borges, I want to forget all about him."

That first conversation ended when he said, with the sincerity of a child, "You may win your heart's desire, but in the end you're cheated of it by death." Then he told us he was expected somewhere. He saw Flo and me and the professor to the door and said he hoped I'd call and see him again about the book. He even offered to phone me. "I don't see why it has to end with one meeting," he said.

Three nights later I was back in the same apartment, this time with a tape recorder. Borges began to reminisce about the Argentine poet Lugones. "Lugones was a very fine craftsman, eh? He was the most important literary man of his country. He boasted of being the most faithful husband in South America, then he fell in love with a mistress and his mistress fell in love with his friend." I mentioned that he had dedicated his book *El hacedor* (translated with the title *Dreamtigers*) to Lugones.

"I think that's the best thing I've done, eh? I mean the idea that I'm speaking to Lugones and then suddenly the reader is made aware that Lugones is dead, that the library is not my library but Lugones's library. And then, after I have created and destroyed that, then I rebuild it again by saying that, after all, I suppose my time will come and then in a sense we'll be contemporaries, no? I think it's quite good, eh? Besides, I think it's good because one feels that it is written with emotion, at least I hope so. I mean you don't think of it as an exercise, no?"

I answered by saying that I understood and admired his idea, but that in my book I wanted a clear picture of Borges and did not want to confuse him with anyone. I added that as he says in "The Aleph," "Our minds are porous with forgetfulness," and I was already becoming conscious of falsifying through my memory all that he had said to me. Then I asked him if I could tape record our conversations. "Yes, you can if you want to, only don't make me too conscious of it, eh?"

For the next six months I worked on this book, taping our conversations whenever possible, and as we progressed a pattern began to appear, certain themes and motifs kept recurring. Of course, the book involved more than merely conducting the interviews. I reread Borges, I attended his class on Argentine Literature at Harvard when I could and his series of six Charles Eliot Norton lectures at Sanders Theatre. The lectures were well attended and very well received. Borges had created genuine excitement in the Cambridge intellectual community. I know this meant a great deal to him. "The kind of cheering I got and what I felt behind it is new to me; I've lectured in Europe and South America, but nothing like this has ever happened to me. To have a new experience when you are seventy is quite a thing."

In the middle of December, around the time of her birthday, Flo, who had seen Borges several times on her own, decided to have a dinner party for him and his wife, to be held in my sister's Cambridge apartment. Borges came with his wife and his personal secretary, John Murchison, a Harvard graduate student. Except for the guests of honor, everyone at the party was under twenty-five. This made no difference to Borges, who has always had a marvelous rapport with the young. Later a hippie unexpectedly dropped in on us, but no one, least of all Borges, was upset. "I wonder what the root word of the hippie is?" he said. His wife thought the young man's appearance was fascinating. Flo had fixed a delicious, authentic Brazilian dinner, complete with the guitar music of Villa-Lobos in the background, and Borges thoroughly enjoyed it. On the way back to his apartment he told me he thought Cambridge was "a very lovable city."

After his successful poetry reading at Harvard (where Robert Lowell introduced him, saying, "It would be impertinent for me to praise him. For many years I've thought he should have won the Nobel Prize"), I decided that I simply had to arrange a similar affair at Brandeis. With the help of Professor Lida of the Spanish department, who is a friend and devoted admirer of Borges, we set a date for April 1. When I told Borges he said, "Well, I hope it's not all a huge practical joke." Then he asked me if I thought twenty or thirty people might show up. It turned out that over five hundred attended (about a fourth of the school's population) and every seat in one of the university's biggest auditoriums was filled twenty minutes before the programme began.

Downstairs, below the auditorium, Borges was nervously going over what he wanted to say about each poem. This in turn made me nervous, but once he sensed my nervousness, he began joking with me, quite spontaneous jokes really, until we had both calmed down. I had the honour of introducing him, and Mr. Murchison and one of Borges's translators, Norman Thomas di Giovanni, read the poems in translation, after which Borges would comment for two or three minutes about each poem. As I led him onstage, I thought how terrifying it must be for a blind person to face and talk to such a large audience. But once he was onstage, Borges's nervousness vanished. He spoke with a fluency that constantly rose to eloquence. The audience was overwhelmed. When I called him the next day and congratulated him again, he seemed upset and cross with himself. "I always make such a fool of myself."

"But how can you say that?" I said. "Everybody loved it."

"Because I feel it, I feel that I acted like a fool."

By the time of his last lecture at Harvard, Borges was the literary hero of Cambridge. I understand that wherever he went in the country, giving his lectures and poetry readings, his reception was equally enthusiastic. In Cambridge, writers like Robert Lowell, Robert Fitzgerald, Yves Bonnefoy, John Updike and Bernard Malamud attended his lectures and lined up to meet him. John Barth said Borges was the man "who had succeeded Joyce and Kafka."

Borges's response to his long overdue success in America

was one of delight and gratefulness, yet he remained, as he will always remain, the most humble and gracious of men. I remember the day I came to see him at the larger and brighter apartment he had just moved in to. After ringing his bell, I hesitated in the lobby, a lobby that seemed like a labyrinth to me, with hallways going in every direction and cryptic numbers with arrows underneath them on each wall. But Borges had anticipated my difficulty and, with the aid of his cane, had walked down three flights of stairs to help me find my way. I was touched, but felt terrible that he had come all the way downstairs on my account. Borges smiled and extended his hand.

—Richard Burgin

A childhood of books; blindness and time; metaphysics;
Cervantes; memory; early work; mirrors and appearances ...

BURGIN: Was there ever a time when you didn't love literature?

BORGES: No, I always knew. I always thought of myself as a writer, even before I wrote a book. Let me say that even when I had written nothing, I knew that I would. I do not think of myself as a good writer, but I knew that my destiny or my fate was a literary one, no? I never thought of myself as being anything else.

BURGIN: You never thought about taking up any career? I mean, your father was a lawyer.

BORGES: Yes. But after all, he had tried to be a literary man and failed. He wrote some very nice sonnets. But he thought that I should fulfill that destiny, no? And he told me not to rush into print.

BURGIN: But you were published when you were pretty young. About twenty.

BORGES: Yes, I know, but he said to me, "You don't have to be in a hurry. You write, you go over what you've written, you destroy, you take your time. What's important is that when you publish something you should think of it as being pretty good, or at least as being the best that you can do."

BURGIN: When did you begin writing?

BORGES: I began when I was a little boy. I wrote an English handbook ten pages long on Greek mythology, in very clumsy English. That was the first thing I ever wrote.

BURGIN: You mean "original mythology" or a translation?

BORGES: No, no, no, no, no. It was just saying, for example, well, "Hercules attempted twelve labors" or Hercules killed the Nemean Lion."

BURGIN: So you must have been reading those books when you were very young.

BORGES: Yes, of course, I'm very fond of mythology. Well, it was nothing, it was just a, it must have been some fifteen pages long ... with the story of the Golden Fleece and the Labyrinth and Hercules—he was my favourite—and then something about the loves of the gods, and the tale of Troy. That was the first thing I ever wrote. I remember it was written in a very short and crabbed handwriting because I was very shortsighted. That's all I can tell you about it. In fact, I think my mother kept a copy for some time, but as we've travelled all over the world, the copy got lost, which is as it should be, of course, because we thought nothing whatever about it, except for the fact that it was being written by a small boy. And then I read a chapter or two of *Don Quixote*, and then, of course, I tried to write archaic Spanish. And that saved me from trying to do the same thing some fifteen years afterwards, no? Because I had already attempted that game and failed at it.

BURGIN: Do you remember much from your childhood?

BORGES: You see, I was always very shortsighted, so when I think of my childhood, I think of books and the illustrations in books. I suppose I can remember every illustration in *Huckleberry Finn* and *Life on the Mississippi* and *Roughing It* and so on. And the illustrations in the *Arabian Nights*. And Dickens—Cruikshank and Fisk illustrations. Of course, well, I also have memories of being in the country, of riding horseback in the estancia on the Uruguay River in the Argentine pampas. I remember my parents and the house with the large patio and so on. But what I chiefly seem to remember are small and minute things. Because those were the ones that I could really see. The illustrations in the encyclopedia and the dictionary, I remember them quite well. *Chambers Encyclopaedia* or the American edition of the *Encyclopaedia Britannica* with the engravings of animals and pyramids.

BURGIN: So you remember the books of your childhood better than the people.

BORGES: Yes, because I could see them.

BURGIN: You're not in touch with any people that you knew from your childhood now? Have you had any lifelong friends?

BORGES: Well, some school companions from Buenos Aires and then, of course, my mother, she's ninety-one; my sister who's three years, three or four years, younger than I am, she's a painter. And then, most of my relatives—most of them have died.

BURGIN: Had you read much before you started to write or did your writing and reading develop together?

BORGES: I've always been a greater reader than a writer. But, of course, I began to lose my eyesight definitely in 1954, and since then I've done my reading by proxy, no? Well, of course, when one cannot read, then one's mind works in a different way. In fact, it might be said that there is a certain benefit in being unable to read, because you think that time flows in a different way. When I had my eyesight, then if I had to spend say a half an hour without doing anything, I would go mad. Because I had to be reading. But now, I can be alone for quite a long time, I don't mind long railroad journeys, I don't mind being alone in a hotel or walking down the street, because, well, I won't say that I am thinking all the time because that would be bragging.

I think I am able to live with a lack of occupation. I don't have to be talking to people or doing things. If somebody had gone out, and I had come here and found the house empty, then I would have been quite content to sit down and let two or three hours pass and go out for a short walk, but I wouldn't feel especially unhappy or lonely. That happens to all people who go blind.

BURGIN: What are you thinking about during that time—a specific problem or . . .

BORGES: I could or I might not be thinking about anything, I'd just be living on, no? Letting time flow or perhaps looking back on memories or walking across a bridge and trying to remember favourite passages, but maybe I wouldn't be doing anything, I'd just be living. I never understand why people say they're bored because they have nothing to do. Because sometimes I have nothing whatever to do, and I don't feel bored. Because I'm not doing things all the time, I'm content.

BURGIN: You've never felt bored in your life?

BORGES: I don't think so. Of course, when I had to be ten days lying on my back after an operation I felt anguish, but not boredom.

BURGIN: You're a metaphysical writer and yet so many writers like, for example, Jane Austen or Fitzgerald or Sinclair Lewis, seem to have no real metaphysical feeling at all.

BORGES: When you speak of Fitzgerald, you're thinking of Edward Fitzgerald, no? Or Scott Fitzgerald?

BURGIN: Yes, the latter.

BORGES: Ah, yes.

BURGIN: I was just naming a writer who came to mind as having essentially no metaphysical feeling.

BORGES: He was always on the surface of things, no? After all, why shouldn't you, no?

BURGIN: Of course, most people live and die without ever, it seems, really thinking about the problems of time or space or infinity.

BORGES: Well, because they take the universe for granted. They take things for granted. They take themselves for granted. That's true. They never wonder at anything, no? They don't think it's strange that they should be living. I remember the first time I felt that was when my father said to me, "What a queer thing," he said, "that I should be living, as they say, behind my eyes, inside my head, I wonder if that makes sense?" And then, it was the first time I felt that, and then instantly I pounced upon that because I knew what he was saying. But many people can hardly understand that. And they say, "Well, but where else could you live?"

BURGIN: Do you think there's something in people's minds that blocks out the sense of the miraculous, something maybe inherent in most human beings that doesn't allow them to think about these things? Because, after all, if they spent their time thinking about the miracle of the universe, they wouldn't do the work civilization depends on and nothing, perhaps, would get done.

BORGES: But I think that today too many things get done.

BURGIN: Yes, of course.

BORGES: Sarmiento wrote that he once met a gaucho and the gaucho said to him, "The countryside is so lovely that I don't want to think about its cause." That's very strange, no? It's a kind of non sequitur, no? Because he should have begun to think about the cause of that beauty. But I suppose he meant that he drank all those things in, and he felt quite happy about them, and he had no use for thinking. But generally speaking, I think men are more prone to metaphysical wondering than women. I think that women take the world for granted. Things for granted. And themselves, no? And circumstances for granted. I think circumstances especially.

BURGIN: They confront each moment as a separate entity

without thinking about all the circumstances that lead up to it.

BORGES: No, because they think of . . .

BURGIN: They take things one at a time.

BORGES: Yes, they take them one at a time, and then they're afraid of cutting a poor figure, or they think of themselves as being actresses, no? The whole world looking at them and, of course, admiring them.

BURGIN: They do seem to be more self-conscious than men on the whole.

BORGES: I have known very intelligent women who are quite incapable of philosophy. One of the most intelligent women I know, she's one of my pupils; she studies Old English with me, well, she was wild over so many books and poets, then I told her to read Berkeley's dialogues, three dialogues, and she could make nothing of them. And then I gave her a book of William James, some problems of philosophy, and she's a very intelligent woman, but she couldn't get inside the books.

BURGIN: They bored her?

BORGES: No, she didn't see why people should be poring over things that seemed very simple to her. So I said, "Yes, but are you sure that time is simple, are you sure that space is simple, are you sure that consciousness is simple?" "Yes," she said. "Well, but could you define them?" She said, "No, I don't think I could, but I don't feel puzzled by them." That, I suppose, is generally what a woman would say, no? And she was a very intelligent woman.

BURGIN: But, of course, there seems to be something in your mind that hasn't blocked out this basic sense of wonder.

BORGES: No.

BURGIN: In fact, it's at the centre of your work, this astonishment at the universe itself.

BORGES: That's why I cannot understand such writers as Scott Fitzgerald or Sinclair Lewis. But Sinclair Lewis has more humanity, no? I think besides that he sympathizes with his victims. When you read *Babbitt*, well, perhaps I think in the end, he became one with Babbitt. For as a writer has to write a novel, a very long novel with a single character, the only way to keep the novel and hero alive is to identify with him. Because if you write a long novel with a hero you dislike or a character that you know very little about, then the book falls to pieces. So, I suppose, that's what happened to Cervantes in a way. When he began *Don Quixote* he knew very little about him and then, as he went on, he had to identify himself with Don Quixote, he must have felt that, I mean, that if he got a long distance from his hero and he was always poking fun at him and seeing him as a figure of fun, then the book would fall to pieces. So that, in the end, he *became* Don Quixote. He sympathized with him against the other creatures, well, against the Innkeeper and the Duke, and the Barber, and the Parson, and so on.

BURGIN: So you think that remark of your father's heralded the beginning of your own metaphysics?

BORGES: Yes, it did.

BURGIN: How old were you then?

BORGES: I don't know. I must have been a very young child. Because I remember he said to me, "Now look here; this is something that may amuse you," and then, he was very fond of chess, he was a good chess player, and then he took me to the chessboard, and he explained to me the paradoxes of Zeno, Achilles and the Tortoise, you remember, the arrows, the fact that movement was impossible because there was always a point in between, and so on. And I remember him speaking of these things to me and I was very puzzled by them. And he explained them with the help of a chessboard.

BURGIN: And your father had aspired to be a writer, you said.

BORGES: Yes, he was a professor of psychology and a lawyer.

BURGIN: And a lawyer also.

BORGES: Well, no, he was a lawyer, but he was also a professor of psychology.

BURGIN: Two separate disciplines.

BORGES: Well, but he was interested in psychology and he had no use for the law. He told me once that he was quite a good lawyer but that he thought the whole thing was a bag of tricks and that to have studied the Civil Code he may as well have tried to learn the laws of whist or poker, no? I mean they were conventions and he knew how to use them, but he didn't believe in them. I remember my father said to me something about memory, a very saddening thing. He said, "I thought I could recall my childhood when we first came to Buenos Aires, but now I know that I can't." I said, "Why?" He said, "Because I think that memory"—I don't know if this was his own theory, I was so impressed by it that I didn't ask him whether he found it or whether he evolved it—but he said, "I think that if I recall something, for example, if today I look back on this morning, then I get an image of what I saw this morning. But if tonight, I'm thinking back on this morning, then what I'm really recalling is not the first image, but the first image in memory. So that every time I recall something, I'm not recalling it really, I'm recalling the last time I recalled it, I'm recalling my last memory of it. So that really," he said, "I have no memories whatever, I have no images whatever, about my childhood, about my youth. And then he illustrated that, with a pile of coins. He piled one coin on top of the other and said, "Well, now this first coin, the bottom coin, this would be the first image, for example, of the house of my childhood. Now this second would be a memory I had of that house when I went to Buenos Aires. Then the third one another memory and so on. And as in every memory there's a slight distortion, I don't suppose that my memory of today ties in with the first images I had," so that, he said, "I try not to think of things in the past because if I do I'll be thinking back on those memories and not on the actual images themselves." And then that saddened me. To think maybe we have no true memories of youth.

BURGIN: That the past was invented, fictitious.

BORGES: That it can be distorted by successive repetition. Because if in every repetition you get a slight distortion, then in the end you will be a long way off from the issue. It's a saddening thought. I wonder if it's true, I wonder what other psychologists would have to say about that.

BURGIN: I'm curious about some of your early books that haven't been translated into English, such as *Historia de la eternidad* (History of Eternity). Are you still fond of those books?

BORGES: No, I think, as I said in the foreword, that I would have written that book in a very different way. Because I think I was very unfair to Plato. Because I thought of the archetypes as being, well, museum pieces, no? But really, they should be thought of as living, as living, of course, in an everlasting

life of their own, in a timeless life. I don't know why, but
when I first read *The Republic*, when I first read about the
types, I felt a kind of fear. When I read, for example, about
the Platonic Triangle, that triangle was to me a triangle by
itself, no? I mean it didn't have three equal sides, two equal
sides, or three unequal sides. It was a kind of magic triangle
made of all those things, and yet not committed to any one
of them, no? I felt that the whole world of Plato, the world of
eternal beings, was somehow uncanny and frightening. And
then what I wrote about the kennings, that was all wrong,
because afterwards when I went into Old English, and I made
some headway in Old Norse, I saw that my whole theory of
them was wrong. And then, in this last book, *Nueva antología
personal* (A Second Personal Anthology), I have added a new
article saying that the idea of kennings had come from the
literary possibilities discovered in compound words. So that
virtually there are very few metaphors, but people remember the metaphors because they're striking. They forget that
when writers, at least in England, began to use kennings, they
thought of them chiefly as rather pompous compound words.
And then they found the metaphorical possibilities of those
compound words.

BURGIN: What about *A Universal History of Infamy*?

BORGES: Well, that was a kind of—I was head editor of a
very popular magazine.

BURGIN: *Sur*?

BORGES: Yes. Coeditor. And then I wrote a story, I changed it greatly, about a man who liberated slaves and then sold them in the South. I got that out of Mark Twain's *Life on the Mississippi*, and then I invented circumstances and I made a kind of story of it. But all the stories in that book were kind of jokes or fakes. But now I don't think very much of that book; it amused me when I wrote it, but I can hardly recall who the characters were.

BURGIN: Would you like *Historia de la eternidad* to be translated, do you think?

BORGES: With due apologies to the reader, yes, explaining that when I wrote that I was a young man and that I made many mistakes.

BURGIN: How old were you when you wrote that?

BORGES: I think I must have been about twenty-nine or thirty, but I matured, if I ever did mature, very, very slowly. But I think I had the luck to begin with the worst mistakes, literary mistakes, a man can make. I began by writing utter rubbish. And then when I found it out I left that kind of rubbish behind. The same thing happened to my friend, Bioy Casares.[1] He's a very intelligent man, but at first every book he published bewildered his friends, because the books were quite pointless, and very involved at the same time. And he

1   Noted Argentinian writer, close friend and collaborator of Borges.

said that he had done his best to be straightforward but that every time a book came out it was a thorn in the flesh, because we didn't know what to say to him about it. And then suddenly he began writing very fine stories. But his first books are so bad that when people come to his house (he's a rich man) and conversation is flagging, then he goes to his room and he comes back with one of his old books. Of course, he, well, he hides what the book is, no? And then he says, "Look here, I got this book from an unknown writer two or three days ago; let's see what we can make of it?" And then he reads it, and then people begin to chuckle and they laugh and sometimes he gives the joke away and sometimes he doesn't, but I know that he's reading his own old stuff and that he thinks of it as a joke. He even encourages people to laugh at it, and when somebody suspects, they will remember, for example, the name of a character and so on, they'll say, "Well, look here, you wrote that," then he says, "Well, really I did, but after all, it's rubbish; you shouldn't think that I wrote it, you should enjoy it for the fun of it."

You see what a nice character he is, no? Because I don't think many people would do that kind of thing. I would feel very bashful. I would have to be apologizing all the time, but he enjoys the joke, a joke against himself. But that kind of thing is very rare in Buenos Aires. In Colombia it might be done, but not in Buenos Aires, or in Mexico, eh? Because in Mexico they take themselves in deadly earnest, and in Buenos Aires also. To suggest, for example, that perhaps—you know that we have a national hero called José de San Martín, you may have heard of him, no? The Argentine Academy of

History decided that no ill could be spoken of him. I mean he was entitled to a reverence denied to the Buddha or to Dante or to Shakespeare or to Plato or to Spinoza, and that was done quite seriously by grown-up men, not by children. And then I remember a Venezuelan writer wrote that San Martín "Tenía un aire avieso." Now *avieso* means "sly," but rather the bad side, no? And then Capdevila, a good Argentine writer, refuted him in two or three pages, saying that those two words, *avieso*—sly, cunning, no?—and San Martín, were impossible, because you may as well speak of a square triangle. And then he very gently explained to the other that that kind of thing was impossible. Because to an Argentine mind—he said nothing whatever about a universal mind—the two words were nonsensical. And now, isn't that very strange; he seems to be a lunatic behaving that way.

BURGIN: What about your book *Evaristo Carriego*?

BORGES: Well, therein a tale hangs. Evaristo Carriego, as you may have read, was a neighbor of ours, and I felt that there was something in the neighbourhood of Palermo—a kind of slum then, I was a boy, I lived in it—I felt that somehow, something might be made out of it. It even had a kind of wistfulness, because there were childhood memories and so on. And then Carriego was the first poet who ever sang the Buenos Aires slums, and he lived on our side of the woods in Palermo. And I remembered him because he used to come to dinner with us every Sunday. I said, "I'll write a book about him." And then my mother very wisely said to me, "After all," she said, "the only reason you have for writing about Carriego is that he was a friend of your father's, and a neighbor and that he died of lung disease in 1921. But why don't you, since you have a year"—because I had won some literary prize or other—"why not write about a really interesting Argentine poet, for example, Lugones."

"No," I said, "I think I can do something better with Carriego," but as I went on writing the book, after I had written my first chapter, a kind of mythology of Palermo, after I had written that first chapter and I had, well, I had begun reading deeply into Carriego, I felt that my mother was right, that after all he was a second-rate poet and I suppose if you get to the end of the book—I suppose a few people have because it's quite a short book—you feel that the writer has lost all interest in the subject and he's doing everything in a very perfunctory kind of way.

BURGIN: It seems that you began to use your famous image of the labyrinth when you first wrote your handbook on Greek mythology, but I wonder how and when you began to use another of your favourite images, the image of a mirror?

BORGES: Well, that, that also goes with the earliest fears and wonders of my childhood, being afraid of mirrors, being afraid of mahogany, being afraid of being repeated. There are some allusions to mirrors in *Fervor de Buenos Aires*, but the feeling came from my childhood. But, of course, when one begins writing, one hardly knows where to find the essential things. Look here, has this girl gone?

BURGIN: Yes.

BORGES: Well, that's right. She's crazy, this girl.

BURGIN: Why, what happened?

BORGES: Well, this morning she came; I was in Hiller's Library. Then, all the time she was aiming that machine at me. And I found out that she has had thirty-six shots and then she popped in a moment ago and wanted to have seventeen more.

BURGIN: What is she doing with them? Is this for herself, or for any magazine?

BORGES: No, she says that perhaps she'll send them to a magazine. She doesn't know. Thirty-six shots, no?

BURGIN: You and di Giovanni were working on the translations?

BORGES: Yes, we were working, yes, but I felt rather, well, I can't be expected to speak or to talk when anyone is around like that.

BURGIN: She was doing them about five inches away from your face?

BORGES: Yes, it was almost a physical assault. Yes, I felt that, I don't know, that somebody had been aiming a revolver at me, no? That she had been aiming a pistol at me, and she kept on at it. Then di Giovanni had the strange idea to tell her to go to Buenos Aires and there she might find other people to photograph and then she got very interested in the idea.

BURGIN: She wants to make a book of photographs of writers, is that it?

BORGES: Writers, yes.

BURGIN: Of course, a camera is a kind of a mirror.

BORGES: Yes.

BURGIN: A permanent mirror.

BORGES: Because I'm afraid of mirrors, maybe I'm afraid of cameras.

BURGIN: You didn't look at yourself much when you could see?

BORGES: No, I never did. Because I never liked being photographed. I can't understand it.

BURGIN: Yet your appearance is always very scrupulous. You always dress very well and look very well.

BORGES: Do I?

BURGIN: Yes, of course. I mean you're always very well groomed and attired.

BORGES: Oh, really? Well, that's because I'm very absent-minded, but I don't think of myself as a dandy or anything like that. I mean I try to be as undistinguished and as invisible as possible. And then, perhaps, the one way to be undistinguished is to dress with a certain care, no? What I mean to say is that when I was a young man I thought that by being careless people wouldn't notice me. But on the contrary. They noticed that I never had my hair cut, that I rarely shaved, no?

BURGIN: You were always this way, even when you were younger?

BORGES: Always. I never wanted to draw attention to myself.

*The living labyrinth of literature; some major work; Nazis;
detective stories; ethics, violence, and the problem of time . . .*

BURGIN: Your writing always, from the first, had its source in
other books?

BORGES: Yes, that's true. Well, because I think of reading a
book as no less an experience than travelling or falling in love.
I think that reading Berkeley or Shaw or Emerson, those are
quite as real experiences to me as seeing London, for example. Of course, I saw London through Dickens and through
Chesterton and through Stevenson, no? Many people are apt
to think of real life on the one side, that means toothache,
headache, travelling and so on, and then you have on the
other side, you have imaginary life and fancy and that means
the arts. But I don't think that that distinction holds water.
I think that everything is a part of life. For example, today I
was telling my wife, I have travelled, well, I won't say all over
the world, but all over the west, no? And yet I find that I have
written poems about out-of-the-way slums of Buenos Aires, I
have written poems on rather drab street corners. And I have
never written poems on a great subject, I mean on a famous
subject. For example, I greatly enjoy New York, but I don't
think I would write about New York. Maybe I'll write about

some street corner, because after all so many people have done that other kind of thing.

BURGIN: You wrote a poem about Emerson, though, and Jonathan Edwards and Spinoza.

BORGES: That's true, yes. But in my country writing about Emerson and Jonathan Edwards is writing perhaps about rather secret characters.

BURGIN: Became they're occult, almost.

BORGES: Yes, more or less. I wrote a poem about Sarmiento because I had to and because I love him, but really I prefer minor characters or if not if I write about Spinoza and Emerson or about Shakespeare and Cervantes, they are major characters, but I write about them in a way that makes them like characters out of books, rather than famous men.

BURGIN: The last time I was here we were talking about your latest book in English, *A Personal Anthology*. Those pieces you decided not to include in it you relegated to a kind of mortality, for yourself anyway. Do you feel you're your own best critic?

BORGES: No, but I believe that some of my pieces have been over-rated. Or, perhaps, I may think that I can let them go their way because people are already fond of them, no? So, I don't have to help them along.

BURGIN: For example, "The Theologians." You didn't want to include that?

BORGES: Did I include that?

BURGIN: No, you didn't.

BORGES: Yes, but there the reason was different. The reason was that although I liked the story, I thought that not too many people would like it.

BURGIN: A concession to popular taste.

BORGES: No, but I thought that since these stories are going to be read by people who may not read the other books, I'll try—and besides, people are always saying that I'm priggish and hard and that is something that is very mazy about me—I'll do my best not to discourage them, no? Instead, I'll help them along. But if I offer them a story like "The Theologians," then they'll feel rather baffled, taken aback, and that may scare them away.

BURGIN: Was that how you felt about "Pierre Menard"—was that why you also excluded it from *A Personal Anthology*?

BORGES: You know, that was the first story I wrote. But it's not wholly a story . . . it's a kind of essay, and then I think that in that story you get a feeling of tiredness and skepticism, no?

Because you think of Menard as coming at the end of a very long literary period, and he comes to the moment when he finds that he doesn't want to encumber the world with any more books. And that, although his fate is to be a literary man, he's not out for fame. He's writing for himself and he decides to do something very, very unobtrusive, he'll rewrite a book that is already there, and very much there, *Don Quixote*. And then, of course, that story has the idea, what I said in my first lecture here, that every time a book is read or reread, then something happens to the book.

BURGIN: It becomes modified.

BORGES: Yes, modified, and every time you read it, it's really a new experience.

BURGIN: Since you see the world's literature as constantly changing, as continuously being modified by time, does this make you feel a sense of futility about creating so-called original works of literature?

BORGES: But not only futility. I see it as something living and growing. I think of the world's literature as a kind of forest, I mean it's tangled and it entangles us but it's growing. Well, to come back to my inevitable image of a labyrinth, well it's a living labyrinth, no? A living maze. Perhaps the word labyrinth is more mysterious than the word maze.

BURGIN: Maze is almost too mechanical a word.

BORGES: Yes, and you feel the "amazement" in the word. With labyrinth you think of Crete and you think of the Greeks. While in maze you may think of Hampton Court, well, not very much of a labyrinth, a kind of toy labyrinth.

BURGIN: What about "Emma Zunz," a story of a living labyrinth?

BORGES: It's very strange, because in a story like "The Immortal" I did my best to be magnificent, while the story "Emma Zunz" is a very drab story, a very grey story, and even the name Emma was chosen because I thought it particularly ugly, but not strikingly ugly, no? And the name Zunz is a very poor name, no? I remember I had a great friend named Emma and she said to me, "But why did you give that awful girl my name?" And then, of course, I couldn't say the truth, but the truth was that when I wrote down the name Emma with the two *m*'s and Zunz with the two *z*'s I was trying to get an ugly and at the same time a colourless name, and I had quite forgotten that one of my best friends was called Emma. The name seems so meaningless, so insignificant, doesn't it sound that way to you?

BURGIN: But one still feels compassion for her, I mean, she is a kind of tool of destiny.

BORGES: Yes, she's a tool of destiny, but I think there's something very mean about revenge, even a just revenge, no? Something futile about it. I dislike revenge. I think that the only

possible revenge is forgetfulness, oblivion. That's the only rev-
enue. But, of course, oblivion makes for forgiving, no?

BURGIN: Well, I know you don't like revenge, and I don't
think you lose your temper much either, do you?

BORGES: I've been angry perhaps, well, I'm almost seventy,
I feel I've been angry four or five times in my life, not more
than that.

BURGIN: That's remarkable. You were angry at Perón, certainly.

BORGES: Yes. That was different.

BURGIN: Of course.

BORGES: One day when I was speaking about Coleridge I
remember four students walked into my class and told me
that a decision had been taken by an assembly for a strike and
they asked me to stop my lecturing. And then I was taken
aback and suddenly I found that without knowing it I had
walked from this side of the room to the other, that I was
facing those four young men, telling them that a man may
make a decision for himself but not for other people, and that
were they crazy enough to think that I would stand that kind
of nonsense. And then they stared at me because they were
astounded at my taking it in that way. Of course, I realized

that I was an elderly man, half blind, and they were four hefty, four husky young men, but I was so angry that I said to them, "Well, as there are many ladies here, if you have anything more to say to me, let's go out on the street and have it out."

BURGIN: You said that?

BORGES: Yes, and then, well, they walked away and then I said, "Well, after this interlude, I think we may go on." And I was rather ashamed of having shouted, and of having felt so angry. That was one of the few times in my life that thing has happened to me.

BURGIN: How long ago was this?

BORGES: This must have been some five years ago. And then the same sort of thing happened twice again, and I reacted much in the same way, but afterwards I felt very, very much ashamed of it.

BURGIN: This was a strike against the university?

BORGES: Yes.

BURGIN: What were they striking for?

BORGES: They were striking because there was a strike among the labourers in the port and they thought the students had to join them. But I always think of strikes as a kind of blackmail, no? I wonder what you think about it?

BURGIN: Students are often striking in this country.

BORGES: In my country also. That they should do it is right, but that they should prevent other people from going to classes, I don't understand. That they should try to bully me? And then I said, well if they knock me down, that doesn't matter, because, after all, the issue of a fight is of no importance whatever. What is important is that a man should not let himself be bullied, don't you think so? After all, what happens to him is not important because nobody thinks that I'm a prizefighter or that I'm any good at fighting. What is important is that I should not let myself be bullied before my students, because if I do, they won't respect me, and I won't respect myself.

BURGIN: Sometimes values, then, are even more important than one's well-being?

BORGES: Oh yes, of course. After all, one's well-being is physical. As I don't think physical things are very real—of course they are real, if you fall off a cliff. That's quite real, no? But in that case I felt that whatever happened to me was quite trifling, utterly trifling. Of course, they were trying to bluff me, because I don't think they had any intention of being violent. But that was one of the few times in my life I've been really angry. And then I was very much ashamed of the fact. I felt that, after all, as a professor, as a man of letters, I shouldn't have been angry, I should have tried to reason with them, instead of that "well, come on and have it out," because after all I was behaving in much the same way as they were.

BURGIN: This reminds me a little bit of "The South."

BORGES: Yes.

BURGIN: I think that's one of your most personal stories.

BORGES: Yes, it is.

BURGIN: The idea of bravery means a lot to you, doesn't it?

BORGES: I think it does because I'm not brave myself. I think if I were really brave it wouldn't mean anything to me. For example, I've been ducking a dentist for a year or so. I'm not personally brave and as my father and my grandfather and my great-grandfather were personally brave men, I mean some of them fell in action . . .

BURGIN: You don't think writing is a kind of bravery?

BORGES: It could be, yes. But perhaps if I were personally brave I wouldn't care so much about bravery. Because, of course, what one cares for is what one hasn't got, no? I mean if a person loves you, you take it for granted, and you may even get tired of her. But if you are jilted, you feel that the bottom is out of the universe, no? But those things are bound to happen. What you really value is what you miss, not what you have.

BURGIN: You say people should be ashamed of anger, but you don't think people should be ashamed of this, of "what to make of a diminished thing?"

BORGES: I don't think one can help it.

BURGIN: Can you help anger?

BORGES: Yes, yes, I think that many people encourage anger or think it a very fine thing.

BURGIN: They think it's manly to fight.

BORGES: Yes, and it isn't, eh?

BURGIN: No. It isn't.

BORGES: I don't think there's anything praiseworthy in anger. It's a kind of weakness. Because really, I think that you should allow very few people to be able to hurt you unless, of course, they bludgeon you or shoot you. For example, I can't understand anybody being angry because a waiter keeps him waiting too long, or because a porter is uncivil to him, or because somebody behind a counter doesn't take him into account because, after all, those people are like shapes in a dream, no?

While the only people who can really hurt you, except in a physical way, by stabbing you or shooting you, are the people you care for. A friend was saying to me, "But you haven't forgiven so and so, and yet you have forgiven somebody who has behaved far worse." I said, "Yes, but so and so was, or I thought he was, a personal friend and so it's rather difficult to forgive him, while the other is an utter stranger so whatever he does, he can't hurt me because he's not that near to me." I mean if you care for people they can hurt you very much, they can hurt you by being indifferent to you, or by slighting you.

BURGIN: You said the highest form of revenge is oblivion.

BORGES: Oblivion, yes, quite right, but, for example, if I were insulted by a stranger in the street, I don't think I would give the matter a second thought. I would just pretend I hadn't heard him and go on, because, after all, I don't exist for him, so why should he exist for me? Of course, in the case of the students walking into my room, walking into my classroom, they knew me, they knew that I was teaching English literature; it was quite different. But if they had been strangers, if they had been, well, brawlers in the street, or drunkards, I suppose I would have taken anything from them and forgotten all about it.

BURGIN: You never got into any fights as a child?

BORGES: Yes, I did. But that was a code. I had to do it. Well, my eyesight was bad, it was very weak and I was generally

defeated. But it had to be done. Because there was a code and,
in fact, when I was a boy, there was even a code of dueling.
But I think dueling is a very stupid custom, no? After all, it's
quite irrelevant. If you quarrel with me and I quarrel with
you, what has our swordsmanship or our marksmanship to do
with it? Nothing—unless you have the mystical idea that God
will punish the wrong. I don't think anybody has that kind
of idea, no? Well, suppose we get back to more . . . because, I
don't know why, I seem to be rambling on.

BURGIN: But this is probably better than anything because it
really enables me to know you.

BORGES: Yes, but it will not be very surprising or very interesting.

BURGIN: I mean, people that write about you all write the
same things.

BORGES: Yes, yes, and they all make things too self-conscious
and too intricate at the same time, no? Don't you think so?

BURGIN: Well, of course it's hard to write about a writer you
like; it's hard to write anyway. You wrote a poem roughly
about that, didn't you? "The Other Tiger."

BORGES: Ah, yes, that one is about the futility of art, no? Or
rather not of art but of art as conveying reality or life. Because, of course, the poem is supposed to be endless, because

the moment I write about the tiger, the tiger isn't the tiger, he becomes a set of words in the poem. "El otro tigre, el que no está en el verso." I was walking up and down the library, and then I wrote that poem in a day or so. I think it's quite a good poem, no? It's a parable also, and yet the parable is not too obvious, the reader doesn't have to be worried by it, or understand it. And then I think I have three tigers, but the reader should be made to feel that the poem is endless.

BURGIN: You'll always be trying to capture the tiger.

BORGES: Yes, because the tiger will always be . . .

BURGIN: . . . outside of art.

BORGES: Outside of art, yes. So it's a kind of hopeless poem, no? The same idea that you get in "A Yellow Rose." In fact, I never thought of it, but when I wrote "The Other Tiger," I was rewriting "A Yellow Rose."

BURGIN: You often speak of stories as echoing other stories you've written before. Was that the case also with "Deutsches Requiem"?

BORGES: Ah, yes. The idea there was that I had met some Nazis, or rather Argentine Nazis. And then I thought that something might be said for them. That if they really held that code of cruelty, of bravery, then they might be, well, of course, lunatics, but there was something epic about them, no? Now, I said, I'll try and imagine a Nazi, not Nazis as they actually are, but I'll try and imagine a man who really thinks that violence and fighting are better than making up things, and peacefulness. I'll do that. And then, I'll make him feel like a Nazi, or the platonic idea of a Nazi. I wrote that after the Second World War because I thought that, after all, nobody had a word to say for the tragedy of Germany. I mean such an important nation. A nation that had produced Schopenhauer and Brahms and so many poets and so many philosophers, and yet it fell victim to a very clumsy idea. I thought, well, I will try and imagine a real Nazi, not a Nazi who is fond of self-pity, as they are, but a Nazi who feels that a violent world is a better world than a peaceful world, and who doesn't care for victory, who is mainly concerned for the *fact* of fighting. Then that Nazi wouldn't mind Germany's being defeated because, after all, if they were defeated, then the others were better fighters. The important thing is that violence should *be*. And then I imagined that Nazi, and I wrote the story. Because there were so many people in Buenos Aires who were on the side of Hitler.

BURGIN: How horrible.

BORGES: It's awful. They were very mean people. But after all, Germany fought splendidly at the beginning of the war. I mean, if you admire Napoleon or if you admire Cromwell, or if you admire any violent manifestation, why not admire Hitler, who did what the others did?

BURGIN: On a much larger scale.

BORGES: On a much larger scale and in a much shorter time. Because he achieved in a few years what Napoleon failed to do in a longer period. And then I realized that those people who were on the side of Germany, that they never thought of the German victories or the German glory. What they really liked was the idea of the blitzkrieg, of London being on fire, of the country being destroyed. As to the German fighters, they took no stock in them. Then I thought, well, now Germany has lost, now America has saved us from this nightmare, but since nobody can doubt on which side I stood, I'll see what can be done from a literary point of view in favour of the Nazis. And then I created that ideal Nazi. Of course, no Nazi was ever like that, because they were full of self-pity; when they were on trial no one thought of saying, "Yes, I'm guilty, I ought to be shot; why not, this is as it should be and I would shoot you if I could." Nobody said that. They were all apologizing and crying because there is something very weak and sentimental about the Germans, something I thoroughly disliked about them. I felt it before, but when I went to Germany I was feeling it all the time. I suppose I told you a conversation I had with a German professor, no?

BURGIN: No, you didn't.

BORGES: Well, I was being shown all over Berlin, one of the ugliest cities in the world, no? Very showy.

BURGIN: I've never been to Germany.

BORGES: Well, you shouldn't, especially if you love Germany, because once you get there you'll begin to hate it. Then I was being shown around Berlin. Of course, there were any number of vacant lots, large patches of empty ground where houses had stood and they had been bombed very thoroughly by the American airmen, and then, you have some German, no?

BURGIN: No, I'm sorry.

BORGES: Well, I'll translate. He said to me, "What have you to say about these ruins?" Then I thought, Germany has started this kind of warfare; the Allies did it because they had to, because the Germans began it. So why should I be pitying this country because of what had happened to it, because *they* started the bombing, and in a very cowardly way. I think Göring told his people that they would be destroying England and that they had nothing whatever to fear from the English airmen. That wasn't a noble thing to say, no? In fact, as a politician he should have said, "We are doing our best to destroy England; maybe we'll get hurt in the process, but it's a risk we have to run"—even if he thought it wasn't that way. So when the professor said to me "What have you to say about these ruins?"—well, my German is not too good, but I had to make my answer very curt, so I said, "I've seen London." And then, of course, he dried up, no? He changed the subject because he had wanted me to pity him.

BURGIN: He wanted a quote from Borges.

BORGES: Well, I gave him a quotation, no?

BURGIN: But not the one he wanted.

BORGES: Not the one he wanted. Then I said to myself, what a pity that I have English blood, because it would have been better if I had been a straight South American. But, after all, I don't think he knew it.

BURGIN: He should have read "Story of the Warrior and the Captive" and then he would have found out.

BORGES: Yes, he would have found out—yes.

BURGIN: That's a good story, don't you think? It's very concise.

BORGES: Yes.

BURGIN: You're able to work in . . .

BORGES: No! I worked in nothing; my grandmother told me the whole thing. Yes, because she was on the frontier and this happened way back in the 1800s.

BURGIN: But you linked it with something that happened in history.

BORGES: With something told by Croce, yes.

BURGIN: And that's what makes it effective.

BORGES: Yes. I thought that the two stories, the two characters, might be essentially the same. A barbarian being wooed
to Rome, to civilization, and then an English girl turning to
witchcraft, to barbarians, to living in the pampas. In fact,
it's the same story as "The Theologians," now that I come to
think of it. In "The Theologians" you have two enemies and
one of them sends the other to the stake. And then they find
out somehow they're the same man. But I think "The Warrior
and the Captive" is a better story, no?

BURGIN: I wouldn't say so, no.

BORGES: No? Why?

BURGIN: There's something almost tragic about "The Theologians." It's a very moving story.

BORGES: Yes, "The Theologians" is more of a tale; the other is
merely the quotation, or the telling, of two parables.

BURGIN: I mean the Theologians are pathetic and yet there's
something noble about them—their earnestness, their self-
importance.

BORGES: Yes, and it's more of a tale. While in the other I think that the tale is spoiled, by the fact of, well, you think of the writer as thinking himself clever, no? In taking two different instances and bringing them together. But "Story of the Warrior and the Captive" makes for easier reading, while most people have been utterly baffled and bored by "The Theologians."

BURGIN: No, I love that story.

BORGES: Well, I love it also, but I'm speaking of my friends, or more of my friends. They all thought that the whole thing was quite pointless.

BURGIN: But I also love "The Garden of Forking Paths," and you don't like that one.

BORGES: I think it's quite good as a detective story, yes.

BURGIN: I think it's more than a detective story, though.

BORGES: Well, it should be. Because, after all, I had Chesterton behind me, and Chesterton knew how to make the most of a detective story. Far more than Ellery Queen or Erle Stanley Gardner. Well, *Ellery Queen*'s quite a good story.

BURGIN: You once edited some anthologies of detective stories, didn't you?

BORGES: I was a director of a series called the Seventh Circle, and we published some hundred and fifty detective novels. We began with Nicholas Blake; we went on to Michael Linnis, then to Wilkie Collins, then to Dickens's *The Mystery of Edwin Drood*, then to different American and English writers, and it had a huge success, because the idea that a detective story could also be literary was a new idea in the Argentine. Because people thought of them, as they must have thought of Westerns, as merely amusing. I think that those books did a lot of good, because they reminded writers that plots were important. If you read detective novels, and if you take up other novels afterwards, the first thing that strikes you—it's unjust, of course, but it happens—is to think of the other books as being shapeless. While in a detective novel everything is very nicely worked in. In fact, it's so nicely worked in that it becomes mechanical, as Stevenson pointed out.

BURGIN: I know you've always tried to avoid seeming mechanical in your fiction and also seeming too spectacular. But I was surprised to hear you say that "The Immortal" was overwritten.

BORGES: Yes, I think I told you that it was too finely written. I feel that you may read the story and miss the point because of the laboured writing.

BURGIN: Was the story perhaps inspired by Swift's immortals in *Gulliver's Travels*?

BORGES: No, because his immortals were very different. They were doddering old things, no? No, I never thought of that. No, I began thinking of the injustice or rather how illogical it was for Christians, let's say, to believe in the immortal soul, and at the same time to believe that what we did during that very brief span of life was important, because even if we lived to be a hundred years old, that's nothing compared to everlastingness, to eternity. I thought, well, even if we live to a hundred, anything we do is unimportant if we go on living, and then I also worked in that mathematical idea that if time is endless, all things are bound to happen to all men, and in that case, after some thousand years every one of us would be a saint, a murderer, a traitor, an adulterer, a fool, a wise man.

BURGIN: The word, or concept, of destiny would have no meaning.

BORGES: No, it would have no meaning. Consequently, in order to make that idea more impressive I thought of Homer forgetting his Greek, forgetting that he had composed the *Iliad*, admiring a not too faithful translation of it by Pope. And then in the end, as the reader had to be made aware that the teller was Homer, I made him tell a confused story where Homer appears not as himself but as a friend. Because, of course, after all that time he was ignorant. And I gave him the name of the wandering Jew Cartaphilus. I thought that helped the tale.

BURGIN: We seem to be talking about violence and also about the problem of time, but that's not unusual, really, since you've often linked these problems, for instance, in a story like "The Secret Miracle."

BORGES: Yes, I think I wrote that during the Second World War. What chiefly interested me—or rather, I was interested in two things. First, in an unassuming miracle, no? For the miracle is wrought for one man only. And then in the idea— this is, I suppose, a religious idea—of a man justifying himself to God by something known only to God, no? God giving him his chance.

BURGIN: A very personal pact between the two.

BORGES: Yes. A personal pact between God and the man, And also, of course, the idea of, well, this is a common idea among the mystics, the idea of something lasting a very short while on earth and a long time in heaven, or in a man's mind, no? I suppose those ideas were behind the tale. Now maybe there are others. And then, as I had also thought out the idea of drama in two acts, and in the first act you would have something very noble and rather pompous, and then in the second act you would find that the real thing was rather tawdry, I thought, "Well, I'll never write that play, but I'll work that idea of the play into a tale of mine." Of course, I couldn't say that Hladík had thought out a drama or a work of art and say nothing whatever about it. Because then, of course, that would fall flat, I had to make it convincing. So, I wove. I interwove those two ideas . . . Now that story has been one of my lucky ones. I'm not especially fond of it, but many people are. And it has even been published in popular magazines in Buenos Aires.

BURGIN: Maybe they think of it as a more optimistic story of yours, in a way . . . It ties in with your ideas on time, your "New Refutation of Time."

BORGES: Yes, yes, and the idea of different times, no? Of different time schemes. Psychological time.

BURGIN: Another story that I would think of in relation to "The Secret Miracle" is "The Other Death"—I mean in the sense that in both tales the hero tries to extend the properties of time, in one by increasing the amount of experience given to man within a unit of time and in the other by reversing time or a man's life in time.

BORGES: Ah! That's one of my best stories, I think. But first I thought of it as a kind of trick story. I felt that I had read about a theologian called Damian, or some such name, and that he thought that all things were possible to God except to undo the past, and then Oscar Wilde said that Christianity made that possible because if a man forgave another he *was* undoing the past. I mean, if you have acted wrongly and that act is forgiven you, then the deed is undone. But I thought I had read a story about a past thing being undone.

My first idea was very trivial. I thought of having chessmen inside a box, or pebbles, and of their position being changed by a man thinking about it. Then I thought this is too arid, I don't think anybody could be convinced by it, and then I thought, well, I'll take a cue from Conrad and the idea of *Lord Jim*, Lord Jim who had been a coward and who wanted to be a brave man, but I'll do it in a magical way.

In my story, you have an Argentine gaucho, among Uruguayan gauchos, who's a coward and feels he should redeem himself, and then he goes back to the Argentine, he lives in a lonely way and he becomes a brave man to himself. And in the end he had undone the past. Instead of running away from that earlier battle in one of the civil wars in Uruguay, he undoes the past, and the people who knew him after the battle, after he had been a coward, forget all about his cowardice, and the teller of the story meets a colonel who had fought in that war and remembers him dying as a brave man should. And the colonel also remembers an unreal detail that is worked in on purpose—he remembers that the man got a bullet wound through the chest. Now, of course, if he had been wounded and fallen off his horse, the other wouldn't have seen where he was wounded.

BURGIN: This feeling of wanting to undo something or to change something in the past also gets into "The Waiting."

BORGES: Well, that happened. No, because the story, well, of course, I can't remember what the man felt at the end, but the idea of a man who went into hiding and was found out after a long time, this happened. It happened, I think it was a Turk and his enemies were also Turks. But I thought that if I worked in Turks, the reader would feel, after all, that I knew little about them. So I turned him into an Italian, because in Buenos Aires everybody is more or less Italian, or is supposed to know a lot about them. Besides, as there are Italian secret societies, the story was essentially the same. But if I'd given it the real Turkish-Egyptian setting, then the reader would have been rather suspicious of me, no? He would have said, "Here is Borges writing about Turks, and he knows little or nothing about them." But if I write about Italians, I'm talking about my next-door neighbours. Yes, as everybody in Buenos Aires is more or less Italian; it makes me feel I'm not really Argentine because I have no Italian blood. That makes me a bit of a foreigner.

BURGIN: But what I meant was this idea of regret, which is essentially a metaphysical regret that we feel against an inevitable destiny, I mean, that feeling is in a lot of your stories. For example, "The South" or "The House of Asterion." Speaking of "The House of Asterion," I understand you wrote that in a single day.

BORGES: Yes. I wrote that in a single day. Because I was editor of a magazine, and there were three blank pages to be filled, there was no time. So I told the illustrator, I want you to work a picture more or less on these lines, and then I wrote the story. I wrote far into the night. And I thought that the whole point lay in the fact of the story being told by, in a sense, the same scheme as "The Form of the Sword," but instead of a man you had a monster telling the story. And also I felt there might be something true in the idea of a monster wanting to be killed, needing to be killed, no? Knowing itself masterless. I mean, he knew all the time there was something awful about him, so he must have felt thankful to the hero who killed him.

Now during the Second World War, I wrote many articles on the war, and in one of them I said that Hitler would be defeated because in his heart of hearts he really wanted defeat. He knew that the whole scheme of Nazism and world empire, all that was preposterous, or perhaps he might have felt that the tragic ending was a better ending than the other, because I don't think that Hitler could have believed in all that stuff about the Germanic race and so on.

Favourite stories; insomnia; a changing picture; Alice in
Wonderland; Ulysses; *Robert Browning; Henry James and
Kafka; Melville . . .*

BURGIN: You seem to disapprove of or criticize so much of
your writing. Which of your stories, say, are you fond of?

BORGES: "The South" and that new story I told you about,
called "The Intruder." I think that's my best story. And then
"Funes the Memorious" isn't too bad. Yes, I think that's quite
a good story. And perhaps "Death and the Mariner's Compass" is a good story.

BURGIN: "The Aleph" isn't one of your favourite stories?

BORGES: "The Aleph," yes, and "The Zahir." "The Zahir"
is about an unforgettable twenty-cent coin. I wonder if you
remember it.

BURGIN: Of course. I remember.

BORGES: And I wrote that out of the word "unforgettable,"
inolvidable, because I read somewhere, "You should hear so-
and-so act or sing, he or she's unforgettable." And I thought,
well what if there were really something unforgettable.

Because I'm interested in words, as you may have noticed. I said, well, let's suppose something really unforgettable, something that you couldn't forget even for a split second. And then, after that, I invented the whole story. But it all came out of the word "unforgettable," *inolvidable*.

BURGIN: In a sense that's a kind of variation on "Funes the Memorious" and even "The Immortal."

BORGES: Yes, but in this case it had to be one thing. And then, of course, that thing had to be something very plain, because if I speak of an unforgettable sphinx or an unforgettable sunset, that's too easy. So I thought, well, I'll take a coin because, I suppose, from the mint you get millions and millions of coins all alike, but let's suppose that one of them is, in some hidden way, unforgettable, and the man sees that coin. He's unable to forget it and then he goes mad. That will give the impression that the man was mad and that was why he thought the coin was unforgettable, no? So the story could be read in two slightly different ways. And then I said, "Well, we have to make the reader believe the story, or at least suspend his disbelief, as Coleridge said." So if something had happened to him before he saw the coin, for example, if a woman he loved had died, that might make it easier for the reader and for myself. Because I can't have the teller of the story buying a package of cigarettes and getting an unforgettable coin. I have to give him some circumstance, to justify what happened to him.

BURGIN: And so you did.

BORGES: Yes. But those stories go together. "Zahir" is one of the names of God, I think. I got it out of Lang's *Modern Egyptians*, I think, or perhaps out of Burton.

BURGIN: The story "Funes the Memorious" is, among other things, about insomnia.

BORGES: About insomnia, yes. A kind of metaphor.

BURGIN: I take it, then, you've had insomnia.

BORGES: Oh, yes.

BURGIN: I have also.

BORGES: Do you?

BURGIN: I don't any more, but I have had it. It's a terrible thing, isn't it?

BORGES: Yes. I think there's something awful about sleeplessness.

BURGIN: Because you think it will never end.

BORGES: Yes, but one also thinks, or rather one feels, that it's not merely a case of being sleepless, but that somebody's *doing* that to you.

BURGIN: A kind of cosmic paranoia.

BORGES: Cosmic paranoia, or some fiendish foe, no? You don't feel it's an accident. You feel that somebody is trying to kill you in a sense, or to hurt you, no?

BURGIN: How long did you have it?

BORGES: Oh, about a year. In Buenos Aires, of course, it's worse than having it here. Because it goes with the long summer nights, with the mosquitoes, with the fact of tossing about in your bed, having to turn your pillow over and over again. In the cold country I think it's easier, no?

BURGIN: No sleeping pills there?

BORGES: Oh yes, I had sleeping pills also, but after a time they did me no good. And then there was a clock. It worried me very much. Because without a clock you may doze off, and then you may try to humbug yourself into thinking that you've slept a long time. If you have a clock, then it will give you the time in the face every quarter of the hour, and then you say, "Well, now it's two o'clock, now it's a quarter past, now half past two, now quarter to three, now the three strokes," and then you go on and on . . . it's awful. Because you know you haven't missed any of the strokes.

BURGIN: What finally got you over the insomnia?

BORGES: I can hardly remember it, because I had sleeping pills and I also went to another house where there were no

clocks, and then I could humbug myself into the belief that I
had slept. And finally, I did sleep. But then I saw a doctor; he
was very intelligent about it. He told me, "You don't have to
worry about sleeplessness because even if you are not sleeping
you are resting, because the mere fact of resting, of being in
bed, of the darkness, all those things are good for you. So that
even if you can't sleep, you don't have to worry." I wonder if
it's a true argument, but, of course, that's hardly the point;
the fact is that I did my best to believe in it, and then, once I
got over that, that after all a sleepless night meant nothing, I
went to sleep quite easily. After a time, of course, as one tends
to forget one's painful experiences, I can't tell you what the
details were of that period. Is there another tale or poem you
want to talk about?

BURGIN: What about the story "The South"? Now you've
said that story is your personal favourite. Do you still feel
that way?

BORGES: But I think I've written a better story called "La
intrusa" ("The Intruder") and you'll find that story in the last
edition of *El Aleph* or of *A Personal Anthology*. I think that's
better than the other. I think that's the best story I ever wrote.
There's nothing personal about it; it's the story of two hoodlums. The intruder is the woman who comes into the lives of
two brothers who are hoodlums. It isn't a trick story. Because
if you read it as a trick story, then, of course, you'll find that
you know what's going to happen at the end of the page or so,
but it isn't meant to be a trick story. On the contrary. What I

was trying to do was to tell an inevitable story so that the end shouldn't come as a surprise.

BURGIN: That's sort of like "The South," though. The sense of inevitability in the story.

BORGES: Yes, yes. But, I think that "La intrusa" is better, because it's simpler.

BURGIN: When did you write it?

BORGES: I wrote it about a year or so ago, and I dedicated it to my mother. She thought that the story was a very unpleasant one. She thought it awful. But when it came to the end there was a moment when one of the characters had to say something, then my mother found the words. And if you read the story, there's a fact I would like you to notice. There are three characters and there is only one character who speaks. The others, well, the others say things and we're told about them. But only one of the characters speaks directly, and he's the one who's the leader of the story. I mean, he's behind all the facts of the story. He makes the final decision, he works out the whole thing, and in order to make that plainer, he's the only character whose voice we hear, throughout the story.

BURGIN: Is it a very short story?

BORGES: Yes, five pages. I think it's the best thing I've done.

Because, for example, in "Hombre de la esquina rosada," I rather overdid the local colour and I spoiled it. But here I think you find, well, I won't say local colour, but you feel that the whole thing happened in the slums around Buenos Aires, and that the whole thing happened some fifty or sixty years ago. And yet, there's nothing picturesque about it. There are, of course, a few Argentine words, but they are not used because they are picturesque but because they are the exact words, no? I mean, if I used any other, I would make the whole thing phony.

BURGIN: What about "Death and the Compass"? Do you like the way you treat the local colour in that story?

BORGES: Yes, but in "Death and the Compass," the story is a kind of nightmare, no? It's not a real story. While in "La intrusa" things are awful, but I think that they are somehow real, and very sad also.

BURGIN: You've quoted Conrad as saying that the real world is so fantastic that it, in a sense, *is* fantastic, there's no difference.

BORGES: Ah, that's wonderful, eh? Yes, it's almost an insult to the mysteries of the world to think that we could invent anything or that we needed to invent anything. And the fact that a writer who wrote fantastic stories had no feeling for the complexity of the world. Perhaps in the foreword to a story called "The Shadow Line," a very fine story in Everyman's

Library—I think he wrote a foreword to that story—there you'll find the quote. Because, you see, people asked him whether "The Shadow Line" was a fantastic story or a realistic story, and he answered that he did not know the difference. And that he would never try to write a "fantastic" story because that would mean he was insensitive, no?

BURGIN: I'm curious also about the story "Tlön, Uqbar, Orbis Tertius."

BORGES: One of the best stories I ever wrote, eh?

BURGIN: You didn't include it in your *Personal Anthology*.

BORGES: No, because a friend of mine told me that many people thought of me as writing cramped and involved tales and she thought that since the real aim of the book was to bring readers nearer to me, it might on the whole be wiser if that story was left out. Because though she liked the story, she thought that it conveyed the wrong idea about me. That it would scare people away from reading the other stories. She said, "For this *Personal Anthology*, you want to make things easier for the reader. While if you give him, well, such a mouthful, you may scare him away and he won't read any of the others." Perhaps the only way to make people read "Tlön, Uqbar, Orbis Tertius" is to make them read other stories first. In Buenos Aires, I mean there are many people who write well, but most of them are trying their hand at realistic stories, no? So this kind of story, of course, falls outside the common expected. That's why I left it out, but it's one of my best stories, perhaps.

BURGIN: You work in your friend Casares again.

BORGES: Yes, well, yes, that's a kind of stock joke we have of working in imaginary and real people in the same story. For example, if I quote an apocryphal book, then the next book to be quoted is a real one, or perhaps an imaginary one, by a real writer, no? When a man writes he feels rather lonely, and then he has to keep his spirits up, no?

BURGIN: Of course, it must be much more difficult for you to write now because of your blindness.

BORGES: It's not difficult, it's impossible. I have to limit myself to short pieces. Yes, because I like to go over what I write; I'm very shaky about what I write. So before I used to write any amount of rough drafts, but now, as I can't do them, I have to imagine drafts. So then, walking up and down the streets or walking up and down the National Library, I think what I want to write, but, of course, they have to be short pieces because otherwise, if I want to see them all at once—that can't be done with long texts. I try to shorten them as much as I can, so I write sonnets, stories maybe one or two pages long. The last thing I wrote, rather a long short story, well, it was six pages.

BURGIN: "La intrusa."

BORGES: "La intrusa," yes. I don't think I'll ever go any farther than that. No, I don't think I'll be able to do it. I want to see at one glance what I've done . . . that's why I don't believe in the novel because I believe a novel is as hazy to the writer as to the reader. I mean a writer writes maybe a chapter, then another, then another one, and in the end he has a kind of bird's eye view of the whole thing, but he may not be very accurate.

BURGIN: Have you written anything since you've been in America?

BORGES: I wrote some quite short pieces; I've written two sonnets, not too good ones, and then a poem about a friend who had promised us a picture. He died. He's a well-known Argentine painter, Larco, and then I thought of the picture he had promised us, promised my wife and me—I met him in the street—and then I thought that in a sense he had given us a picture because he had intended to do so, and so the picture was in some mystic way or other with us, except that the picture was perhaps a richer picture because it was a picture that kept growing and changing with time and we could imagine it in many different ways, and then in the end I thanked him for that unceasing, shifting picture, saying that, of course, he wouldn't find any place on the four walls of a room, but still he'd be there with us. That was more or less the plot of the poem. I wrote that in a kind of prose poem.

BURGIN: That's very nice.

BORGES: Well, I wander. Now, when I was in New York, I began writing a poem and then I realized it was the same poem I had written to my friend all over again, yes, because it was snowing and we were on the, I don't know, sixteenth floor of one of those New York towers, and then I lay there, it was snowing very hard, we were practically snowed in, snow-bound, because we couldn't walk, and then I felt that somehow the mere fact of being in the heart of New York and of knowing that all those complex and beautiful buildings were around us, that mere fact made us see them and possess them better than if we had been gaping at shop windows or other sights, no? It's the same idea, of course. And suddenly I realized that I'd been going over the same ground, the idea of having something because you don't have it or because you have it in a more abstract way.

BURGIN: This seems to be the type of feeling one gets from a story like "The Circular Ruins." Can you tell me what the pattern was behind the story?

BORGES: No. I can't say much about the conception, but I can tell you that when I wrote that story the writing took me a week. I went to my regular business. I went to—I was working at a very small and rather shabby public library in Buenos Aires, in a very grey and featureless street. I had to go there every day and work six hours, and then sometimes I would meet my friends, we would go and see a film, or I would have dinner with somebody, but all the time I felt that life was unreal. What was really near to me was that story I was writing. That's the only time in my life I've had that feeling, so that story must have meant something—to me.

BURGIN: Have you ever read any poetry by Wallace Stevens?

BORGES: I seem to recall the name in some anthology. Why? Is there something akin to it?

BURGIN: I think he believes a lot in the integrity of the dreamer, in the integrity of the life of the imagination as opposed to the physical universe.

BORGES: Yes, well, but I don't think that feeling got into the story, it was merely a kind of intensity I had. That story came from the sentence "And I let off dreaming about you"—in *Alice in Wonderland*.

BURGIN: You like *Alice in Wonderland*, don't you?

BORGES: Oh, it's a wonderful book! But when I read it, I don't think I was quite as conscious of its being a nightmare book and I wonder if Lewis Carroll was. Maybe the nightmare touch is stronger because he wasn't aware of it, no? And it came to him from something inner.

I remember as a child I, of course, I gently enjoyed the book, but I felt that there was—of course, I never put this feeling into words—but I felt something eerie, something uncanny about it. But now when I reread it, I think the nightmare touches are pretty clear. And perhaps, perhaps Lewis Carroll disliked Sir John Tenniel's pictures, well, they're pen-and-ink drawings in the Victorian manner, very solid, and perhaps he thought, or he felt rather, that Sir John Tenniel had missed the nightmare touch and that he would have preferred something simpler.

BURGIN: I don't know if I believe in pictures with a book. Do you?

BORGES: Henry James didn't. Henry James didn't because he said that pictures were taken in at a glance and so, of course, as the visual element is stronger, well, a picture makes an impact on you, that is, if you see, for example, a picture of a man, you see him all at once, while if you read an account of him or a description of him, then the description is successive, The illustration is entire, it is, in a certain sense, in eternity, or rather in the present. Then he said what was the use of his describing a person in forty or fifty lines when that description was blotted by the illustration. I think some editor or other proposed to Henry James an illustrated edition and first he wouldn't accept the idea, and then he accepted it on condition that there would be no pictures of scenes, or of characters. For the pictures should be, let's say, around the text, no?—they should never overlap the text. So he felt much the same way as you do, no?

BURGIN: Would you dislike an edition of your works with illustrations?

BORGES: No, I wouldn't, because in my books I don't think the visual element is very important. I would like it because I don't think it would do the text any harm, and it might enrich the text. But perhaps Henry James *had* a definite idea of what his characters were like, though one doesn't get that idea. When one reads his books, one doesn't feel that he, that he could have known the people if he met them in the street. Perhaps I think of Henry James as being a finer storyteller than he was a novelist. I think his novels are very burdensome to read, no? Don't you think so? I think his novels are very . . . James was a great master of situations, in a sense, of his *plot*, but his characters hardly exist outside the story. I think of his characters as being unreal. I think that the characters are made—well, perhaps, in a detective story, for example, the characters are made for the plot, for the sake of the plot, and that all his long analysis is perhaps a kind of fake, or maybe he was deceiving himself.

BURGIN: What novelists do you think could create characters?

BORGES: Conrad, and Dickens, Conrad certainly, because in Conrad you feel that everything is real and at the same time very poetical, no? I should put Conrad as a novelist far above Henry James. When I was a young man I thought Dostoevsky was the greatest novelist. And then after ten years or so, when I reread him, I felt greatly disappointed. I felt that the characters were unreal and that also the characters were part of a plot. Because in real life, even in a difficult situation, even when you are worrying very much about something, even when you feel anguish or when you feel hatred—well, I've never felt hatred—or love or fury maybe, you also live along other lines, no? I mean, a man is in love, but at the same time he is interested in the cinema, or he is thinking about mathematics or poetry or politics, while in novels, in most novels, the characters are simply living through what's happening to them. No, that might be the case with very simple people, but I don't see, I don't think that happens.

BURGIN: Do you think a book like *Ulysses*, for example, was, among other things, an attempt to show the full spectrum of thought?

BORGES: Yes, but I think that *Ulysses* is a failure, really. Well, by the time it's read through, you know thousands and thousands of circumstances about the characters, but you don't know them. And if you think of the characters in Joyce, you don't think of them as you think of the characters in Stevenson or in Dickens, because in the case of a character, let's say in a book by Stevenson, a man may appear, may last a page, but you feel that you know him or that there's more in him to be known, but in the case of *Ulysses* you are told thousands of circumstances about the characters. You know, for example, well, you know that they went twice to the men's room, you know all the books they read, you know their exact positions when they are sitting down or standing up, but you don't really know them. It's as if Joyce had gone over them with a microscope or a magnifying glass.

BURGIN: I imagine you've revealed a lot about English literature to your students.

BORGES: Nobody knows a lot about English literature, it's so rich ... But I believe, for example, that I have revealed Robert Browning to many young men in Buenos Aires who knew nothing whatsoever about him. Now I'm wondering if Browning, instead of writing poetry—of course he should have written poetry—but I think that many of Browning's pieces would have fared better, at least as far as the reader goes, had they been written as short stories. For example, I think that he wrote some very fine verses in *The Ring and the Book*. We find it burdensome because I suppose we've grown out of the habit of reading long poems in blank verse. But had he written it in prose, had *The Ring and the Book* been written as a novel, and the same story told over and over again by different characters, he might have been more amusing, no? Though he would have lost many fine passages of verse. Then I should think of Robert Browning as the forerunner of all modern literature. But nowadays we don't, because we're put off by the ...

BURGIN: ... poetic technicalities.

BORGES: Yes, the poetic technicalities, by the blank verse, by the rather artificial style. But had he been, let's say, well, yes, had he been a good prose writer, then I think that we should think of Browning as being the forerunner of what is called modern literature.

BURGIN: Why do you say that?

BORGES: Because when I told the plots of his poems to my students, they were wild about them. And then, when they read them, they found them, well, a task. But if you tell somebody the framework of *The Ring and the Book*, it's very interesting. The idea of having the same story told by different characters from different angles, that seems to be, well, more or less, what Henry James would have liked to do—a long time before Henry James. I mean that you should think of Browning as having been the forerunner, quite as good as the forerunner, of Henry James or of Kafka. While today we don't think of him in that way, and nobody seems to be reading him, except out of duty, but I think people should enjoy reading him.

BURGIN: You've linked Henry James and Kafka before—you seem to associate them in your mind for some reason.

BORGES: I think that there is a likeness between them. I think that the sense of things being ambiguous, of things being meaningless, of living in a meaningless universe, of things being many-sided and finally unexplained; well, Henry James wrote to his brother that he thought of the world as being a diamond museum, a museum of monsters. I think that he must have felt life in much the same way.

BURGIN: And yet the characters in James or in Kafka are always striving for something definite. They always have definite goals.

BORGES: They have definite goals, but they never attain them. I mean, when you've read the first page of *The Trial* you know that he'll never know why he's being judged, why he's being tried, I mean; in the case of Henry James, the same thing happens. The moment you know that the man is after the Aspern papers, you know, well, either that he'll never find the papers, or that if he does find them, they'll be worthless. You may feel that.

BURGIN: But then it's more a sense of impotence than it is an ambiguity.

BORGES: Of course, but it's also an ambiguity. For example, "The Turn of the Screw." That's a stock example. One might find others. "The Abasement of the Northmores"—the whole story is told as a tale of revenge. And, in the end, you don't know whether the revenge will work out or not. Because, after all, the letters of the widow's husband, they may be published and nothing may come of them. So that in the end, the whole story is about revenge, and when you reach the last page, you do not know whether the woman will accomplish her purpose or not. A very strange story . . . I suppose that you prefer Kafka to Henry James?

BURGIN: No, they stand for different things for me.

BORGES: But do they?

BURGIN: You don't seem to think so. But I think that Henry

James believed in society; he never really questioned the social order.

BORGES: I don't think so.

BURGIN: I think he accepted society. I think that he couldn't conceive of a world without society and he believed in man and, moreover, in certain conventions. He was a student of man's behaviour.

BORGES: Yes, I know, but he believed in them in a desperate way, because it was the only thing he could grasp.

BURGIN: It was an order, a sense of order.

BORGES: But I don't think he felt happy.

BURGIN: But Kafka's imagination is far more metaphorical.

BORGES: Yes, but I think that you get many things in James that you don't get in Kafka. For example, in Henry James you are made to feel that there *is* a meaning behind experience, perhaps too many meanings. While in Kafka, you know that he knew no more about the castle or about the judges and the trial than you do. Because the castle and the judges are symbols of the universe, and nobody is expected to know anything about the universe. But in the case of Henry James, you think that he might have had his personal theories or you feel that he knows more of what he's talking about. I mean that though his stories may be parables of the subject, still they're not written by him to be parables. I think he was really very interested in the solution, maybe he had two or three solutions and so in a sense I think of Henry James as being far more complex than Kafka, but that may be a weakness. Perhaps the strength of Kafka may be in his lack of complexity.

BURGIN: I think of James as being able to create characters, whereas Kafka has no characters. Kafka is closer to poetry really. He works with metaphors and types as opposed to characters.

BORGES: No, there are no characters.

BURGIN: But James could create characters.

BORGES: Are you sure of that?

BURGIN: You don't seem to think so.

BORGES: No, I think that what is interesting in James are the situations more than the characters. Let's take a very obvious example. If I think of Dickens, I'm thinking of Sir Pickwick, Pip, David Copperfield. I think of people, well, I might go on and on. While if I think of James, I'm thinking about a situation and a plot. I'm not thinking about people. I'm thinking about what happened to them. If I think about *What Maisie Knew*, I think of the framework of a hideous story of adultery being told by a child who cannot understand. I think of that and not of Maisie herself and not of her parents or of her mother's lover and so on.

BURGIN: You also said that you don't think *Ulysses* has any real characters either.

BORGES: No.

BURGIN: What do you think of when you think of that book? The language perhaps?

BORGES: Yes, I think of it as being verbal. I think I said that we know thousands of things about Daedalus or about Bloom, but I don't think we know them. At least I don't. But I think I know quite a lot about the characters in Shakespeare or in Dickens. Now—I'll qualify this, I suppose you can help me out—in the case of *Moby-Dick*, I think that I believe in the story rather than in the characters, because the whole story is a symbol, the white whale stands for evil, and Captain Ahab stands, I suppose, for the wrong way of doing battle against evil, but I cannot believe in him personally. Can you?

BURGIN: To think only in terms of an allegory or a symbol seems reductive of the text; it reduces the story of one of its elements.

BORGES: Yes, of course it does. That's why Melville said that the book was not an allegory, no?

BURGIN: But I don't think it's so specific that you can say the whale stands for evil; maybe the whale stands for many things—you feel many things, but you can't perhaps verbalize the exact thing that the whale stands for. I mean, I don't like to think of it in terms of algebra, where one thing equals another.

BORGES: No, no, of course the idea of the whale is richer than the idea of evil.

BURGIN: Yes.

BORGES: Of course, I'm not allowed to see the work in Melville's mind, but you think of Captain Ahab as being more complex than any abstract statement.

BURGIN: Yes. Ahab has presence, he has real presence on the page, but I don't really think of him as a real man.

BORGES: I think of Billy Budd as being a real man.

BURGIN: Yes.

BORGES: And Benito Cereno—but in the case of *Moby-Dick*, the whole thing is so overloaded with gorgeous language, no?

BURGIN: Shakespearean, almost.

BORGES: Shakespearean and Carlylean also, no? Because you feel that Carlyle is in Melville.

BURGIN: What about "Bartleby the Scrivener"—did you like that story?

BORGES: Yes, I remember an anthology that came out in Buenos Aires, well, about six months ago. Six Argentine writers could choose the best story they knew. And one of those writers took that story, "Bartleby."

BURGIN: The best story of Melville or the best story by anybody?

BORGES: I mean by anybody.

BURGIN: One story from all of world literature, that's very difficult.

BORGES: Yes, but I don't think the aim was really to find out the best stories in the world by any means. I think what they wanted was to get an anthology that people might want to buy, no? That people might be interested in. Then one took "Bartleby," and one took, I don't know why, a very disagreeable and rather bogus story by Lovecraft. Have you read Lovecraft?

BURGIN: No, I haven't.

BORGES: Well, no reason why you should. And somebody had a story about a mermaid by Hans Andersen, I suppose you know it. Well, it's not a very good story.

BURGIN: Strange choices.

BORGES: Then somebody had a short Chinese story, quite a good story—three pages long. And then, I wonder what you will make of my choice? I took Hawthorne's "Wakefield," about the man who stays away from home all those years. Well, strangely enough, there were six stories and three by American authors: Melville, Lovecraft and Hawthorne.

BURGIN: Did you have a hard time picking Hawthorne from the others or did you know it right away?

BORGES: No. Well, of course, I really wasn't thinking of all the stories I know. And it had to be a story already translated into Spanish. That limited my choice. Besides, as I didn't want to astonish people, because I think that to take a story by Lovecraft and to say it's the best story in the world, that's done in order to amaze people. Because I don't think that anybody would think that Lovecraft wrote the finest story in the world, if the phrase the finest story in the world can have any meaning. I hesitated between the story and some story by Kipling. And then I thought that that story was a very fine story to be written ever so long ago. The book came out and now there is going to be a second series, by different writers, of course. It was a book that sold very well.

BURGIN: Have you had occasion to go to Salem since you've been here?

BORGES: Yes, I went several times to Salem and then I went to Walden also. And I should say that the whole American adventure began here, no? That the history of America began here. In fact, I should say that the West was invented by New Englanders, no?

Tales and meanings; favourite poems; the gifts of unhappiness; a girl from Buenos Aires; Homer; parables . . .

BORGES: You know, I want to tell you that some people have no literary sense. Consequently they think that if anything literary pleases them, they have to look for far-fetched reasons. I mean, for example, instead of saying, "Well, I like this because this is fine poetry, or because this is a story that I follow with interest; I'm really forgetting about myself and I'm thinking of the character," they're trying to think that the whole thing is full of half truths, reasons and symbols. They'll say, "Yes, we enjoyed that tale of yours, but what did you mean by it?" The answer is, "I meant nothing whatever, I meant the tale itself. If I could have said it in plainer words, I would have written it otherwise." But the tale itself should be its own reality, no? People never accept that. They like to think that writers are aiming at something. In fact, I think that most people think—of course they won't say so to themselves or to anybody else—they think of literature as being a kind of *Aesop's Fables*, no? Everything is written to prove something—not for the sheer pleasure of writing it, or for the sheer interest a writer may have in the characters or in the situation or in whatever it may be, no? I think that people are always looking for some kind of lesson, no?

BURGIN: Maybe they hope that books will give them what the world doesn't. They want some meaning. They want truths. They want to be told how to live, from books.

BORGES: Perhaps. But if they thought of poetry as they think of music, that might make things easier for them, don't you think so? When you're hearing music, well, of course, I know nothing whatever about music, I suppose you'd just be pleased or displeased or bored. But if you're reading a book, you're hunting for a book behind the book, no? Consequently you have to invent all kinds of reasons ... Well, maybe you wanted to ask me something far more concrete; I'm just rambling on. But I think that's the only way for a real conversation to begin—by rambling on, no? I'm not looking too closely at what I'm saying.

BURGIN: No, I think what you say is very true. In the colleges, at least in the schools I've gone to, the method is always to explicate things, explain very literally what everything means.

BORGES: I'm thinking, for example, that you might have a very crude character in a skit, a comedy or whatever it might be, talking Shakespeare, "Music to hear, why hear'st thou music sadly? Sweets with sweets war not, joy delights in joy." Now that's very beautiful, very lovely. And yet you might have a very clumsy and very illiterate character, saying, "If you make music, why do you feel sad? And why does it make you sad?" And it would boil down to the same idea, no? But when Shakespeare says it, it's lovely and in the other case, I mean if the thought were plainly expressed, it would give you the idea of a very clumsy kind of person, no? Don't you think so?

BURGIN: Yes, I do.

BORGES: I dislike that kind of thing. And another thing I dislike is if people ask me, for example, "Do you admire Shaw?" "Yes." "Do you admire Chesterton?" "Yes." "And if you had to choose between them?" "But I don't." They stand for different moods, don't you think so? I mean, you might say that Chesterton as a weaver of tales was cleverer than Shaw, but that on the whole I think of Shaw as a wiser man than Chesterton. But I'm not thinking of a kind of duel between them. Why not have both?

BURGIN: Things get back to a duel again. Everyone seems to have to prove he's the best.

BORGES: Well, that's a kind of football mind, no? Or they live a boxing match.

BURGIN: I don't like boxing. Do you?

BORGES: Yes. At least, when I had sight, I enjoyed seeing a boxing match ... but as to football, I know so little about it that I could never tell who was who or who was winning or who was losing. The whole thing seemed meaningless to me, and besides, it's so ugly, the spectacle. While a cockfight— you've seen cockfights, no?

BURGIN: No, I haven't. They're banned in America.

BORGES: Well, they're banned also in my country, but you see them. Besides, a cockfight is a fair fight because both cocks are thoroughly enjoying it, enjoying it, of course, in their own hellish way. I've seen bullfights, also. But to an Argentine, there's something very unfair about a bullfight.

The Spaniards told me that no one thought of danger in a bullfight, because no bullfighters ever run any dangers. They thought of it as sheer technique, and things had to be done in a very elegant way, and that a bullfighter had to be very skillful about it. But that nobody ever thought of a man risking his life, or of a bull being killed, or of the horses being murdered, that those things were not seen. That it was really a game of skill. I said, "Yes, but it's not very skillful to have a bull and some ten or twelve people killing him." "Yes," they said, "because you're thinking of the idea of a fair fight, but the idea of a fight isn't there at all. What is really important is that things should be done in a very deft way; it's a kind of dance." And they said, "I see you don't understand anything about bullfighting if you are thinking of it as a dangerous sport or if you're thinking of a man risking his life."

BURGIN: I think we're constantly trying to block out our distant animal past, and a bullfight is one of the many forms of that idea.

BORGES: It might be that, but not a very fair form. When my father was a boy, he knew a man, or rather, he knew several men whose job it was to kill jaguars. They were called *tigreros* because a jaguar is called a tiger, no? Even though it's smaller. The same thing might be found in Venezuela or in Colombia or in southern Brazil. This was in Buenos Aires, I think.

Well, the man's job was to kill jaguars. He had a pack of dogs with him, he had a poncho (a cloak with a hole in it) and a long knife. The dogs would make the jaguar come from his den. Then the man would hold up the poncho in his left hand, moving it up and down. The jaguar would spring, because the jaguar was a kind of machine; it always did the same thing. The jaguar was the same jaguar over and over again, an everlasting jaguar, no? Then he would jump, and as the poncho could hardly defend the man's hands, his hands were scratched by the claws of the jaguar, but at that moment the jaguar laid himself bare to the man's knife and the man killed him with an upward thrust.

I asked my father if the *tigreros* were especially admired and he said no, they did that job even as other men might be cattle drovers or might break in horses or might do any other job, but it was the one thing they did. And they did it skillfully; after all, there were not too many jaguars and sometimes they led a very lazy kind of life. And then men would find out that the sheep or the cattle had been killed by jaguars and they would call the *tigrero*. The *tigrero* would perform that particular job and go on to his own quiet life again. But nobody thought of him as a hero. He was a man who, well, as you might think of a skillful carpenter, or weaver, or sailor. He was a specialized workman.

BURGIN: And, of course, you wrote a poem about tigers called "The Other Tiger"?

BORGES: Yes.

BURGIN: Do you think you're more gifted in fiction than in poetry or . . .

BORGES: I don't think I'm gifted at all. But I don't think of them as different, or different species or tasks. I find that sometimes my thinking, or rather my fancy, takes the shape of verse and sometimes the shape of prose, and sometimes it may be a tale or it may be a confession or it may be, well, an opinion. But I don't think they are different. I mean, I don't think of them as being in watertight compartments, and I think it's mere chance that a fancy of mine or even an opinion of mine should find its way into prose or into verse. Those things are not essential. You might as well say, you might as well speak about the fact of a book having a grey or a red binding.

BURGIN: In the poem "Matthew 25:30," you say, "And still you have not written the poem." Do you really feel that way?

BORGES: But that was an actual experience. I felt that an overwhelming number of things had happened to me, and among these things bitterness and misfortune and disappointment and sadness and loneliness and that, after all, those things are the stuff that poetry is made of, and that if I were a real poet, I should think of my unhappiness, of my many forms of unhappiness, as being really gifts. And I felt that I hadn't used them. Of course, in the poem there were good things also, no? For example, Walt Whitman, but most of them, at least as far as I can remember the poem, most of them, are really misfortunes. Yet they were all gifts, and the experience was real. When I wrote it, I may have invented the examples I used, but the feeling I had of many things having happened to me and yet of my not having used them for an essential purpose, which to me was poetry, that to me was a very real experience. In fact, it made me forget that that afternoon I had been jilted. Of course, those things happen to all men, no? Yes, of course, all men forsake and are forsaken. But when it happens, it's quite important. Well, I suppose it must have happened to you or if not, it will happen in time.

BURGIN: It has.

BORGES: Well, of course. That's like falling off a horse in my country—everybody does. We're a nation of riders and we all fall off our horses, no?

BURGIN: In a sense then, all men are more alike than they are different.

BORGES: Yes, the same idea. But that poem's quite a good one, yes?

BURGIN: Yes.

BORGES: I think it's quite a fair expression of a true experience, because it really happened to me and it happened in that very place on a railway bridge.

BURGIN: I also love that poem "The Gifts," which takes place in a library.

BORGES: That's a very strange thing—I found out that I was the third director of the library who was blind. Because first there was the novelist José Mármol, who was a contemporary of Rosas. Then there was Groussac who was blind. But when I wrote that, I didn't know anything about Mármol, and that made it easier. Because I think it was better to have only two, no? And then I thought that perhaps Groussac would have liked it, because I was expressing him also. Of course, Groussac was a very proud man, a very lonely one too. He was a Frenchman who was quite famous in the Argentine because he once wrote that "Being famous in South America does not make one less well-known." I suppose he must have felt that way. And yet, somehow, I hope he feels, somewhere, that I was expressing what he must have felt too. Because it's rather obvious, the irony of having so many books at your beck and call and being unable to read them, no?

BURGIN: Do you have someone read to you now?

BORGES: Yes, but it's not the same thing. I was very fond of browsing over books, and if you have a reader, well, you can't make them browse. I mean, they open the book, they go on reading, if you feel a bit bored you can't tell them to skip a few pages, but rather, you try to receive what they're reading you. And the pleasure of walking to a bookshop, of opening books and looking at them and so on, that is denied. I mean I can only ask, "Have you received any new books in Old English or Old Norse?" And then they say no, and then . . .

BURGIN: You walk out?

BORGES: Yes, then I walk out. But before I used to spend perhaps a couple of hours every morning, because there were very fine bookshops in Buenos Aires. Now somehow they've died out. Well, the whole city is decaying.

BURGIN: You think so?

BORGES: Oh yes, we all feel that we are living in a very discouraged, skeptical and hopeless country. Perhaps the only strength our government has lies in the fact that people think that any other government would be quite as bad, no? That doesn't make for real strength.

BURGIN: You once wrote the lines, "To have seen nothing or almost nothing except the face of a girl from Buenos Aires, a face that does not want you to remember it."

BORGES: I wrote that when I was in Colombia. I remember a journalist came to see me, and he asked me several questions about the literary life in Buenos Aires, my own output and so on. Then I said to him, "Look here, could you give me some five minutes of your time?" And he said, he was very polite, and he said "Very willingly." And then I said, "If you could jot down a few lines." And he said. "Oh, of course." And I dictated those lines to him.

BURGIN: They used it as the epilogue in the *Labyrinths* book.

BORGES: Yes.

BURGIN: But the reason I mention that to you, well I don't want to over-explicate, but it seems to say that love is the only thing that man can see or know.

BORGES: Yes, it might mean that, but I think it's not fair to ask that because the way I said it was better, no? But when I was composing that poem, I wasn't thinking in general terms, I was thinking of a very concrete girl, who felt a very concrete indifference. And I felt very unhappy at the time. And, of course, after I wrote it, I felt a kind of relief. Because once you have written something, you work it out of your system, no? I mean, when a writer writes something he's done what he can. He's made something of his experience.

BURGIN: I've been wondering. I know you like "The Gifts" and "The Other Tiger." Do you have any other favourite poems?

BORGES: The poems I've written or the poems I've read?

BURGIN: No, the poems you've written.

BORGES: Yes, I think that quite the best poem is the poem called "El golem." Because "El golem," well, first, Bioy Casares told me it's the one poem where humour has a part. And then the poem is more or less an account of how the golem was evolved, and then there is a kind of parable because one thinks of the golem as being very clumsy, no? And the rabbi is rather ashamed of him. And in the end it is suggested that as the golem is to the magician, to the cabalist, so is a man to God, no? And that perhaps God may be ashamed of mankind as the cabalist was ashamed of the golem. And then I think that in that poem you may also find a parable of the nature of art. Though the rabbi intended something beautiful, or very important, the creation of a man, he only succeeded in creating a very clumsy doll, no? A kind of parody of mankind. And then I like the last verses:

> En la hora de angustia y de luz vaga,
> en su Golem los ojos detenía.
> ¿Quién nos dirá las cosas que sentía
> Dios, al mirar a su rabino en Praga?

> At the hour of anguish and vague light,
> He would rest his eyes on his Golem.
> Who can tell us what God felt,
> As He gazed on His rabbi in Prague?

I think that's one of my best poems. And then another

poem I like that's quite obvious is "Límites." But I think I can give you the reason. The reason is, I suppose, that it's quite easy to write an original poem, let's say, with original thoughts or surprising thoughts. I mean, if you think, that's what the metaphysical poets did in England, no? But in the case of "Límites," I have had the great luck to write a poem about something that everybody has felt, or may feel. For example, what I am feeling today in Cambridge—I am going tomorrow to New York and won't be back until Wednesday or Thursday and I feel that I am doing things for the last time.

And yet, I mean that most common feelings, most human feelings, have found their way into poetry and been worked over and over again, as they should have been, for the last thousand years. But here I've been very lucky, because having a long literary past, I mean, having read in many literatures, I seem to have found a subject that is fairly new and yet a subject that is not thought to be extravagant. Because when I say, especially at a certain age, that we are doing things for the last time and may not be aware of it—for all I know I may be looking out of this window for the last time, or there are books that I shall never read, books that I have already read for the last time—I think that I have opened, let's say, the door to a feeling that all men have. And then, of course, other poets will do far better than I do, but this will be one of the first poems on the subject. So I'm almost as lucky as if I were the first man to write a poem about the joy of spring, or the sadness of the fall or autumn.

BURGIN: And yet it's the same idea as that parable of yours,

"The Witness," where you talk about the infinite number of things that die to the universe with the death of each man.

BORGES: About that Saxon?

BURGIN: Yes. It's the same kind of idea. Which did you write first?

BORGES: No, I think I wrote that parable, that story of the Saxon, first.

BURGIN: So that was really the first time you wrote out the idea.

BORGES: No, the first time I wrote it I attributed it to a bogus Uruguayan poet, Julio Hacolo—you'll find it at the end of the *Obra poética*. That was a rough draft.

BURGIN: Oh, and that preceded the parable and the long poem.

BORGES: Yes. Somehow I knew that I had found something quite good, but at the same time I didn't think anything could be made of it. So I thought, "I'll jot this down, I can't do anything with it beyond a few lines," and I jotted it down, and some ten or fifteen years after I jotted it down, I came to the conclusion that something more could be done, and then I wrote the poem. Now when I published that very short fragment, nobody remarked on it, because they believed in that bogus book I attributed it to. After all, there was a very good subject, waiting to be picked up by anybody. It was read by most of my friends, I mean by most of the literary men in Buenos Aires, and yet they never discovered the literary possibilities. And so I was given ten or fifteen years, and then I worked it out in a poem that became quite, well, notorious, let us say, or famous in a sense.

So I think those two poems are good. And then there's another poem that I like and that no one seems to have remarked on, except one poet in Buenos Aires. No one seems to have read it, a poem called "Una rosa y Milton." It's a poem about the last rose that Milton had in his hand and then I think of Milton holding the rose up to his face, smelling the perfume, and of course he wouldn't be able to tell whether the rose was white or red or yellow. I think that's quite a good poem. Another poem about a blind poet. Homer and Milton. And then I think a poem about the sea is quite good, "El mar."

BURGIN: You mention Homer, and of course, Homer keeps cropping up in your writing. For example, you wrote a parable about him called "The Maker."

BORGES: I think that when I wrote that I felt that there was romantic content in the fact of his being aware of his blindness and, at the same time, aware of the fact that his *Iliad* and his *Odyssey* were coming to him, no?

BURGIN: You often speak of a moment when people find out who they are.

BORGES: Yes, that's it, well, that would have been Homer's moment. And then, also, I suppose I must have felt the same thing that I felt when I wrote that poem about Milton. I must have felt the fact that his blindness, in a sense, was a godsend. Because now, of course, that the world had left him, he was free to discover or to invent—both words mean the same thing—his own world, the world of the epic. I suppose those were the two ideas behind my mind, no? First the idea of Homer being aware of his blindness and at the same time thinking of it as a joy, no? And then the idea, also, that, well, perhaps you lose something but at the same time you get something else, and the something else that you get may be the mere sense of loss but at least something is given to you, no? So, maybe, if you're interested in the parable, I suppose you will find behind the parable, or behind the fable, those three feelings.

BURGIN: You really love Homer, don't you?

BORGES: No, I love *The Odyssey*, but I dislike *The Iliad*. In *The Iliad*, after all, the central character is a fool. I mean, you can't admire a man like Achilles, no? A man who is sulking all the time, who is angry because people have been personally unjust to him, and who finally sends the body of the man he's killed to his father. Of course, all those things are natural enough in those tales, but there's nothing noble in *The Iliad* ... Well, you may find, I think there may be two noble ideas in *The Iliad*. First, that Achilles is fighting to subdue a city which he'll never enter, and that the Trojans are fighting a hopeless battle because they know that ultimately the city will fall. So there is a kind of nobility, don't you think so? But I wonder if Homer felt it in that way?

BURGIN: If I might ask you about one more parable, "Parable of the Palace."

BORGES: Well, the "Parable of the Palace" is really the same parable, the same kind of parable as "The Yellow Rose" or "The Other Tiger." It's a parable about art existing in its own plane but not being given to deal with reality. As far as I can recall it, if the poem is perfect then there's no need for the palace. I mean if art is perfect, then the world is superfluous. I think that should be the meaning, no? And besides, I think that the poet never can cope with reality. So I think of art and nature, well, nature and the world as being two different worlds. So I should say that the "Parable of the Palace" is really the same kind of thinking as you get in a very brief way in "The Yellow Rose" or perhaps in "The Other Tiger." In "The Other Tiger" the subject is more the insufficiency of art, but I suppose they all boil down to the same thing, no? I mean you have the real tiger and "el otro tigre," you have the real palace, and "el otro palacio," they stand for the same thing—for a kind of discord, for the inability of art to cope with the world and, at the same time, the fact that though art cannot repeat nature and may not be a repetition of nature, yet it is justified in its own right.

Literature as pleasure; The Maker; *the literature of literature; a change in direction;* Don Quixote *and Cervantes; Hiroshima; death and the problem of infinity; dissolving reality . . .*

BURGIN: You know, I was thinking of how, during all our talks, you have often emphasized enjoyment, that one should primarily enjoy literature. Do you think pleasure is the main purpose of literature, if it can be said to have a purpose?

BORGES: Well, pleasure, I don't know, but you should get a kick out of it, no?

BURGIN: Yes.

BORGES: Well, if you allow me to attempt slang, yes I think that should be so. You know I'm a professor of English and American literature and I tell my students that if you begin a book, if at the end of fifteen or twenty pages you feel that the book is a task for you, then lay that book and lay that author aside for a time because it won't do you any good. For example, one of my favourite authors is De Quincey. Well, as he's a rather slow-moving author, people somehow don't like him. So I say, well, if you don't like De Quincey then let him alone; my task is not to impose my likes or dislikes on you. What I really want is that you should fall in love with American or English literature, and if you find your way to a few authors or a few authors find their way to you, then that's as it should be. You don't have to worry about dates. And I should advise you to read the book, to read the foreword if you care to, and then you might read an article or so in any old edition of the *Encyclopaedia Britannica*, because the new ones are no good, no? And then take any history of English literature, it might be Andrew Lang, it might be Saintsbury, though I'm not overfond of him, it might be Sampson, though he's intruding his likes and dislikes, but I would say any of those three, though Andrew Lang stops at Swinburne, from Beowulf to Swinburne. Now as to American histories of literature, there's a very amusing book by a man called Lewisohn.

BURGIN: Ludwig Lewisohn?

BORGES: Yes, but of course, his work is based on psychoanalysis and I wonder if you can psychoanalyse Edgar Allan Poe or Nathaniel Hawthorne and Jonathan Edwards, no? I think it's rather late in the day. And if you were a contemporary, it would be far more difficult because you'd have too many facts about them. It's a pity, no, that that whole book is based on what seems to me a wrong approach? And as I say, as to examinations, I won't ask you the dates of an author because then you would ask me and then I would fail. But, of course, I think it's all to the good that you should think of Dr. Johnson as belonging to the eighteenth century and of Milton belonging to the seventeenth, because if not, then you couldn't understand them. Now, as to those birth dates, that may or may not be important. As to the dates of their deaths, as they didn't know them themselves, why should you know them? Why should you know more than the authors did? And as to articles, bibliographies and so on, you don't have to worry about that. What you have to do is to read the authors. Then, as to histories of literature, they are all more or less copies of one another, with variation.

BURGIN: If enjoyment is paramount, then what do you suppose it is that gives one a sense of enjoyment from a book?

BORGES: There may be two opposite explanations to that. The individual is getting away from his personal circumstances and finding his way into another world, but at the same time, perhaps that other world interests him because it's nearer his inner self than his circumstances. I mean, if I, suppose I take one of my favourite authors, Stevenson, if I were to read Stevenson now, I would feel that, as I was reading the book, I wouldn't think of myself as being in England or in South America. I would think I was inside the book. And yet that book might be telling me a secret, or half-guessed-at things about myself. But, of course, those explanations go together, no? If you accept one, you don't have to refuse the other.

BURGIN: Of all the books you've published, do you have a favourite book?

BORGES: Of all my books, yes. The book called *The Maker*,

El hacedor. Yes, because it wrote itself. And my English translator, or my American translator, he wrote to me and said that there was no English word for "El hacedor." And then I wrote him back, saying that "El hacedor" had been translated from the English "The Maker." But, of course, all words in a foreign tongue have a certain distinction behind them, no? So that "El hacedor" meant more to him than "The Maker." But when I used "El hacedor" for the poet, for Homer, I was merely translating the Old English or the Middle English word "maker."

BURGIN: Some people didn't take you seriously when you said that *El hacedor*, translated back into English as *Dreamtigers*, would make all your other books unnecessary. But as I read it, I think more and more that perhaps it was more than a joke on your part—saying that.

BORGES: Well, I know, because the book seems to be slight, but it isn't really slight.

BURGIN: It has all your essential themes and motifs and, more important, your voice.

BORGES: The book may be a slight book, but it isn't a slight book to me, because when I go back to that book, I find that I've said the things I had to say or that I worked out the images I had to work out. And besides, the book has found some favour with the public. It's not a boring book. In fact, it couldn't be because it's so short.

BURGIN: When were the poems that were in that collection written?

BORGES: They were written all through my life. My editor told me, "We want a new book from you; there should be a market for that book." And I said, "I haven't any book." And then my editor said to me, "Oh yes, you have. If you go through your shelves or drawers you'll find odds and ends. Maybe a book can be evolved from them." So I think I remember it was a rainy Sunday in Buenos Aires and I had nothing whatever to do because, well, there was an appointment that had failed. I had my sight, I wasn't blind, so I thought, I'll look over my papers. Maybe I'll find something in my drawers. I found cuttings, old magazines, and then I found that there was the book all ready for me.

BURGIN: Of pieces that you had thought were insignificant before?

BORGES: Yes, and I took them to the editor and said, "I want you to tell me honestly—you don't have to answer me to-day or next week—whether you think this book, this kind of crazy-quilt patchwork, can be published; you take ten days or a fortnight or a month over it, and look it over carefully be-cause I don't want you to be spending money on a book that nobody will buy or that may find some very hard critics." And then he answered me within a week, saying "Yes."

BURGIN: I wanted to ask you about one of your parables in *El hacedor*, your parable about Cervantes.

BORGES: Ah, yes! I'm very interested in Cervantes. I think—I wonder how you feel about it—when I think of English literature I'm attracted to it, among many other things, because when I'm thinking of it, I'm thinking about men more than about books. I think that English literature, like England, is very personal. For example, if I think of Sir Thomas Browne or Doctor Johnson, George Bernard Shaw or John Bunyan, or the men who wrote the Saxon Elegies. I think of them as *men* even as I might think of the many characters in Dickens or in Shakespeare. While I get the sense, of course I may be wrong, I get the sense that when I'm thinking about Spanish literature, I'm thinking about books rather than about men. Really, because of my ignorance. I'm attracted to Cervantes even as I'm attracted to Dickens and Shaw—because I can imagine him. But in the case of other writers, I can hardly imagine them, I think of their books. I wonder, for example, had I the chance to talk to Lope de Vega, I wonder what we would have spoken about.

BURGIN: He wrote eighteen hundred plays, or something like that.

BORGES: Yes, I would think of his plays rather. While if somebody said, "You'll be having supper with Sir Thomas Browne, or even with Doctor Johnson"—of course, he would have been full of sweeping statements—I would have said, "I'll enjoy this evening; I can imagine it." Well, Cervantes is one of the few Spanish authors I can imagine. I know, more or less, what a chat with him would be. I know, for example, how he might apologize for some of the things he's written. How he wouldn't take himself too seriously. I'm sure of it, even as in the case of Samuel Butler or Wells, so one of the reasons why I feel attracted to Cervantes is that I think of him not only as a writer, one of the greatest of novelists, but also as a man. And as Whitman says, "Camerado, this is no book. Who touches this touches a man." But I hardly ever get that feeling with Spanish books, or with Italian books. But I get that feeling, I get it all the time, when I'm reading American or English literature.

BURGIN: But now, I'm curious, you have this parable of Cervantes, and you have written other parables about Dante and Homer and Shakespeare; I was wondering how you got the idea, because I don't know of any other writer who has ever done this. I mean, to have written parables in which you tried to imagine or re-imagine the history of particular compositions or of their authors' lives or destinies?

BORGES: I think the explanation is fairly simple. The explanation is that I am interested in literature, not only for its own sake, but also as one of the many destinies of man. I mean, as I am interested in soldiers and in adventures and in mystics—well, I come from a military family and so on—I am also interested in literary men. I mean, in the fact of a man dedicating himself to his dreams, then trying to work them out. And doing his best to make other people share them. I'm interested in literary life. Of course, I'm not the first writer to do that because there are many Henry James stories about literary subjects, about literary men.

BURGIN: You've really based your whole literature on literature itself in a way.

BORGES: Yes. That may be an argument against my literature, and yet why? In many of my stories and poems the central character is a literary man. Well, this means to say that I think that literature has not only enriched the world by giving it books but also by evolving a new type of man, the man of letters. For example, you might not care for the works of Coleridge; you might think that outside of three or four poems, "The Ancient Mariner," "Christabel," "Kubla Khan," maybe "Time, River, and Imagining," what he wrote is not very interesting, it's very wordy, and very perplexed and perplexing stuff, confused and confusing stuff, and yet I'm sure that you think of Coleridge as you might think of somebody you had known, no? I mean, that though his writing is sometimes rather unreal, yet you think of him as being a real man—perhaps because of his unreality also, and because he lived in a kind of haze world or dream world, no? So that I think literature has enriched the world not only through books, but through a new type of man, the man of letters.

BURGIN: Have you ever tried writing in a more realistic way, basing your stories not on literature but on developed characters and . . .

BORGES: Yes. I have done that.

BURGIN: You did try that first?

BORGES: No, no. I'm going back to that. I wonder if you've seen the last edition of *El Aleph*?

BURGIN: "La intrusa," yes, that's a very atypical story of yours in some ways. But in some ways it isn't.

BORGES: No, but I find that "La intrusa" is a different story from the others. Well, I have several plots of the same kind and when I'm back in Buenos Aires, I'll go on with them.

BURGIN: Why do you suppose you've changed your direction?

BORGES: Well, there might be many reasons. I suppose the real reason is that when I thought of "La intrusa" I was very interested in it and I wrote it down in quite a short time. That might be a reason. And the other reason might be that I feel that the kind of stories you get in *El Aleph* and in *Ficciones* are becoming rather mechanical, and that people expect that kind of thing from me. So that I feel as if I were a kind of high fidelity, a kind of gadget, no? A kind of factory producing stories about mistaken identity, about mazes, about tigers, about mirrors, about people being somebody else, or about all men being the same man or one man being his own mortal foe. And another reason, which may be a rather malicious one, is that there are quite a few people all over the world who are writing that kind of story and there's no reason why I should go on doing it. Especially as some of them do it far better than I do, no?

BURGIN: Well, they followed you, and no, I don't think they do it better or as well. Though, of course, some of your stories, like "The Form of the Sword," are more "realistic."

BORGES: That's one of the stories I like least, because it's a trick story after all. Now a friend of mine told me that he saw through the trick, and I thought that is as it should be because I did think of the story as a trick story. I thought that if the reader felt that the man was talking about himself, it would make the whole thing more "pathetic," but if he were merely telling a story about somebody who betrayed him, then that's a mere episode. But if a traitor in a bashful way found that the only way of telling the story was to think of himself as outside the story, or rather, joining together with the central character, the story might be better and besides it might be said for the story that, well, let's suppose—let's suppose you made me some confession about yourself, no? You told me something that nobody knew or that nobody was supposed to know, or that you wanted hidden and suppose that in the moment you were telling it to me, you felt outside the whole thing because the mere fact of telling it made you the teller and not the told.

BURGIN: I think you underrate that story because, though, as you say, it ends in a trick, an O. Henry kind of reversal, I think that . . .

BORGES: But of course, when I wrote that story I was quite young and then I believed in cleverness, and now I think that cleverness is a hindrance. I don't think a writer should be clever, or clever in a mechanical way, no?

BURGIN: I think it's deeper than the plot. I think it's thematically very interesting and I think it's somewhat akin to that story "The Theologians" because . . .

BORGES: No. "The Theologians" is a better story.

BURGIN: "The Theologians" *is* a better story.

BORGES: But, perhaps, perhaps "The Form of the Sword" makes for easier reading?

BURGIN: Yes, but what I'm saying is that essentially the person who was telling the story could have been either one of the men. Just like in "The Theologians," the two men were the same to God.

BORGES: Yes, that's true. I never thought of that.

BURGIN: He could have been either one of the men, and in a sense he was.

BORGES: I never thought of that. Well, you have enriched the story. Thank you.

BURGIN: You noticed something very interesting about Don

Quixote. That he never does kill a man in all his adventures, although he often engages in fights.

BORGES: Ah, yes! I wonder about that.

BURGIN: And then you wrote that parable.

BORGES: Well, I suppose the real reason or the obvious reason would be that Cervantes wanted to keep within the limits of farce and had he killed a man, then the book, then that would have been too real, no? Don't you think so? I mean if Quixote kills a man, then he somehow is a real, bad man, whether he feels himself justified or not. I don't think Cervantes wanted to go as far as all that, no? He wanted to keep his book within certain bounds, and had Don Quixote killed a man that would have done Cervantes no good.

BURGIN: Also, there's the idea you've mentioned that the author at some time in the book becomes the main character. So perhaps Cervantes couldn't bear to kill a man *himself,* if he *became* Don Quixote.

BORGES: Yes, yet I suppose he must have killed many in his life, as a soldier. But that's different, no? Because if a soldier kills a man, he kills him impersonally, no? Don't you think so? I mean if you kill a man as a soldier you don't really kill him. You're merely a tool. Or somebody else kills him through you or, well, you don't have to accept any responsibility. I don't think a soldier feels guilty about the people he's killed, no? Except the men who threw the bomb on Hiroshima.

BURGIN: Well, some of them have gone insane, some of those people who were involved with the bomb.

BORGES: Yes, but somehow, now I suppose you are—I shouldn't say this to you, I'll be blurting it out.

BURGIN: Well, say it.

BORGES: I can't think of Hiroshima as being worse than any battle.

BURGIN: What do you mean?

BORGES: It ended the war in a day. And the fact that many people are killed is the same fact that one man is killed. Because every man dies his own death and he would have died it anyhow. Then, well, of course, one hardly knows all the people who were killed in Hiroshima. After all, Japan was in favour of violence, of empire, of fighting, of being very cruel; they were not early Christians or anything of the kind. In fact, had they had the bomb, they would have done the same thing to America.

Hold it, I know that I shouldn't be saying these things because they make me seem very callous. But somehow I have never been able to feel that way about Hiroshima. Perhaps something new is happening to mankind, but I think that if you accept war, well, I should say this, if you accept war, you have to accept cruelty. And you have to accept slaughter and bloodshed and that kind of thing. And after all, to be killed by a rifle, or to be killed by a stone thrown at you, or by somebody thrusting a knife into you, is essentially the same. Hiroshima stands out, because many innocent people were involved and because the whole thing was packed into a single moment. But you know, after all, I don't see the difference between being in Hiroshima and a battle or—maybe I'm saying this for the sake of argument—or between Hiroshima and human life. I mean in Hiroshima the whole tragedy, the whole horror, is packed very close and you can see it very vividly. But the mere fact of man growing, and falling sick, and dying is Hiroshima spread out.

You understand what I mean? For example, there's a part in Cervantes and in Quevedo where they speak against firearms, no? Because they say that, after all, a man may be a good marksman and another may not be. No, but what I think is this: I think that really all arms are horrible, no? Are awful. We've grown more or less accustomed, our sensibilities have been blunted, by ages and ages and so we accept a sword. Or we accept a bayonet or a spear, and we accept firearms, but whenever a new arm is about, it seems peculiarly atrocious, though after all, if you are going to be killed, it hardly matters to you whether you are killed by a bomb, or by being knocked on the head, or by being knifed.

Of course, it might be said that war is essentially awful or rather that killing is essentially awful or perhaps that dying is essentially awful. But we have our sensibilities blunted, and when a new weapon appears, we think of it as being especially devilish—you remember that Milton makes the Devil invent gunpowder and artillery, no? Because in those days artillery was sufficiently new to be specially awful. And perhaps a day will come when people will accept the atomic bomb when we shrink from some keener invention.

BURGIN: Then it's a certain idea that you find awful. The idea of a man being killed.

BORGES: Yes, but if you accept that, and war accepts that, or else there would be no war ... the idea of a man fighting a duel is the same idea, essentially.

BURGIN: Well, the soldier may accept it while he's fighting under orders, but I, as an individual, don't have to accept it. And the soldier may not be a person who thinks in terms of accepting something or not; he may just do something because he's told to by his government. He doesn't necessarily question it. Do you think that each soldier debates with himself whether a given war is right or not, or examines the reasons and debates whether it's worth taking another human life?

BORGES: I don't think he has to. I don't think he could do it, no? Yet I remember my great-grandfather, Colonel Suárez, who had fought the War of Independence, the War of Brazil and the Civil War. When he was about to marry, his wife asked him about the men he had killed. And then he told her that he had only killed one man, and that was a Spaniard he had to run through with a lance in order to save a friend of his who had been taken prisoner. He said that was the one man he killed in the War of Independence, the War of Brazil and the Civil War. Now I suspect that he was lying, but that he knew at the same time that she must have felt a kind of horror at the idea that she was going to give herself to a bloodstained man, no? So I suppose he invented that in order to calm her.

You remember, the battle of Junín lasted three quarters of an hour—not a shot was fired, the whole thing was done with spears and swords. It stands to reason that someone was going to get killed, and that he would have known it. And besides, I knew he had many executed. But I suppose that in a sense he felt that what he had done was awful, or rather, perhaps he felt that those things were awful to a woman but not to a man, no? I don't think he was a clear thinker or anything of the kind, but he must have felt what all soldiers feel, well, these things have to be done and I've done them, and I'm not ashamed of it, but why speak of those things to a woman who cannot be expected to understand? I suppose he was lying, because battles, well, they were very primitive in those days and quite small affairs, but the fact that they were primitive and small affairs may, I suppose—if a man killed anybody he had to be quite sure about it, no? Because if you are hacking away with a sword at somebody, you know whether you've killed him or not.

BURGIN: I've always felt that by working out the rational consequences of mystic ideas, you've written about the things people are most astonished at or afraid of, that you've selected things to write about that are really even more terrifying than death, like infinity.

BORGES: But I don't think of death as being terrifying. I was going over a sonnet with di Giovanni and the subject of that sonnet; I began by saying to the reader that he was invulnerable, that nothing could happen to him, that God had given to him the certainty of dust, mortality, and that, after all, if one day he should die, he could always fall back on the fact that life was a mere dream. But I don't think of death as being terrifying.

BURGIN: What about infinity?

BORGES: Infinity, yes, because infinity is an intellectual problem. Death means you stop being, you cease from thinking, or feeling, or wondering, and at least you're lucky in that you don't have to worry. You might as well worry, as the Latin poet said, about the ages, and ages that preceded you when you did not exist. You might as well worry about the endless past as the endless future uninhabited by you ... Infinity, yes, that's a problem, but death isn't a problem in that sense. There's no difficulty whatever in imagining that even as I go to sleep every night, I may have a long sleep at the end. I mean it's not an intellectual problem. I don't understand Unamuno, because Unamuno wrote that God, for him, was the provider of immortality, that he couldn't believe in a God who didn't believe in immortality. I don't see that. There might be a God who might not want me to go on living, or who might think that the universe does not need me. After all, it did not need me until 1899, when I was born. I was left out until it did.

BURGIN: Perhaps a stronger argument against God might be the idea of random happenings. The fact that people can be born as freaks, physical freaks, or that, people can be born paralysed.

BORGES: Oh, yes, of course. In fact, there are many arguments against God, but there are only four arguments for His existence.

BURGIN: Four arguments? Which are they?

BORGES: Well, one is called the ontological argument; it seems to be a mere trick. It runs thus. Can you imagine a perfect being, all powerful, all wise, and so on, and then you say yes, no?

BURGIN: Yes.

BORGES: Now, does that being exist or not?

BURGIN: Well, then the answer is, if you imagine him, he exists.

BORGES: No, no. Then you would say no, I don't know.

BURGIN: You have to say no?

BORGES: Or, I don't know. Then here the argument is clinched, in a very unconvincing way as I see it. You said that you could imagine a perfect being, a being all wise, all knowing; well, if that being does not exist, then it isn't perfect. Because how can a nonexistent being be perfect? So you have to add existence to it. It's not a very convincing argument, no? And then it was made still worse. It went, does God exist? I don't know. Does a man exist? Well, he seems to exist. Then you think that God, who is eternal, omnipotent, and so on, cannot achieve what a man has to start with? And God, who is so wise, cannot even attain to manhood? Well, of course, that's not an argument. In fact, if you say that God cannot succeed in existing, you are really supposing there is existence, no? Because if you don't exist you cannot succeed or fail at it.

BURGIN: Do you think that a lot of philosophy has been wasted arguing about the existence of God, or can you still derive enjoyment from it?

BORGES: I can derive great enjoyment from it, the enjoyment I get out of detective novels or science fiction. Enjoyment of the imagination. But I don't think anybody could take it too seriously. Of course, you may believe in God, I daresay there is a God, but I don't believe in Him because of those arguments. I should say that I believe in God in spite of theology. Theologians follow the rules of the games; you accept certain premises and you have to accept the conclusions.

BURGIN: You once said that if a man is happy, he doesn't want to write or really do anything, he just wants to be.

BORGES: Yes, because happiness is an end in itself. That's one of the advantages, or perhaps the only advantage, of unhappiness. That unhappiness *has* to be transmuted into something.

BURGIN: So then, your own writing proceeds out of a sense of sorrow.

BORGES: I think that all writing comes out of unhappiness. I suppose that when Mark Twain was writing about the Mississippi and about the rafts, I suppose he was simply looking at his own past, no? He had a kind of homesickness for the Mississippi ... Of course, when you're happy you don't need anything, no? Now I can be happy, but not for a long time.

BURGIN: Walt Whitman tried to write some poems about happiness, but we see through them so that ...

BORGES: But Whitman, I think, overdid it. Because in him everything is wonderful, you know? I don't think that anybody could really believe that everything is wonderful, no? Except in a sense of it being a wonder. Of course, you can do without that particular kind of miracle. No, in the case of Whitman I think he thought it was his duty as an American to be happy. And that he had to cheer up his readers. Of course, he wanted to be unlike any other poet, but Whitman worked with a programme, I should say, he began with a theory and then he went on to his work. I don't think of him as a spontaneous writer.

BURGIN: Although he tries to convey the impression of spontaneity.

BORGES: Well, he had to do it.

BURGIN: Do you think any poets are really spontaneous?

BORGES: No, but I think that if you're writing about unhappiness, feeling bleak or discouraged, it can be done more sincerely . . . Somebody wrote, I think it was William Henry Hudson, that he had tried to—I think he was quoting someone else—that he wanted to study philosophy and that he tried to read, well, I don't know, Hume or Spinoza, but he couldn't do it because happiness was always breaking in. He really was just bragging, no? In the case of most people, happiness isn't always breaking in, but if it breaks in, you are thankful for it.

BURGIN: But don't you think many people are ashamed to admit they're happy? In fact, Bertrand Russell wrote a book called *The Right to Be Happy.*

BORGES: Well, because people felt that if other people were unhappy, their happiness would be resented. I don't think we need be afraid of feeling too happy, no? For example, if suddenly, walking down the street or sitting here in my room, I feel happy, I think I'd better accept it and not pry into it.

Because if I pry into it, I shall find that I have far too many reasons for being unhappy. But I think that one should accept happiness, and perhaps unexplained happiness is all to the better because I think that's something right in your body, no? Or in your mind. But if you're happy because of something that has happened, then you may be unhappy the next moment. I mean if you are just being spontaneously, innocently, happy, that's all to the good. Of course, that doesn't happen too often.

BURGIN: You once said to me that you could envision a world without novels, but not without tales or verses. How do you feel about philosophy? Could you envision a world without philosophy?

BORGES: No. I think that people who have no philosophy live a poor kind of life, no? People who are too sure about reality and about themselves. I think that philosophy helps you to live. For example, if you think of life as a dream, there may be something gruesome or uncanny about it, and you may sometimes feel that you are living in a nightmare, but if you think of reality as something hard and fast, that's still worse, no? I think that philosophy may give the world a kind of haziness, but that haziness is all to the good. If you're a materialist, if you believe in hard and fast things, then you're tied down by reality, or by what you call reality. So that, in a sense, philosophy dissolves reality, but as reality is not always too pleasant, you will be helped by the dissolution. Well, those are very obvious thoughts, of course, though they are none the less true for being obvious.

"BORGES AND I"

INTERVIEW BY DANIEL BOURNE, STEPHEN CAPE,
CHARLES SILVER

ARTFUL DODGE, 1980

Jorge Luis Borges is a man of many worlds and moods. A significant figure in modern Spanish literature, he has drawn much of his creative force from the Germanic world: English poetry, Franz Kafka, the warrior mythology of the Old English and Norse. Strongly anti-political and anti-moralistic, this Argentine's work frequently revolves around the history of South America and the stirrings of the human heart. A storyteller who claims to perform his work in a simple manner, Borges may set his tales in exotic temples or in neighborhood bars; he may describe tigers and knives flashing in moonlight, or the patience of a scholar thumbing an ancient manuscript. Borges's writings emerge from dreams and from experience. Nothing can be taken for certain; life is powerful, but poorly glimpsed before it overwhelms.

The result of Borges's continual crossing of linguistic, mythological, and social boundaries is a body of work— essays, tales and poetry—which has earned recognition the world over. In 1960, he shared the World Publisher's Prize with the French playwright Samuel Beckett, and he is often predicted to be a future recipient of the Nobel Prize for Literature. Although Borges began publishing in Buenos Aires in the 1920s, and his important collection of prose, *Ficciones*, came out in 1944, it was not until the appearance in 1961 of *Labyrinths* (New Directions), an anthology of his earlier stories, essays, and poetry, that his work spread to America and other English-speaking lands. A translation of *Ficciones* appeared in 1962, and subsequent translations have included *A Personal Anthology* (1967), *The Aleph and Other Stories* (1972), and *In Praise of Darkness* (1974), the latter four translated by or under the direction of Norman Thomas di Giovanni, with whom Borges worked closely.

To talk closely to Jorge Luis Borges is to track him through a labyrinth of his past experiences and attitudes, and the walls that one encounters in the search might be painted in unexpected ways. These may furnish clues or merely diversions in the pursuit, but to understand Borges at least partially is to realize that these clues and diversions are the *Borges*. We must not expect to find Borges the same each time. There is not one Borges, but many.

This is the Jorge Luis Borges whom the *Artful Dodge* encountered on April 25, 1980.

JORGE LUIS BORGES: First let me say: straightforward questions. Not, for example, "What do you think of the future?" when there are so many futures and quite different from each other, I suppose.

DANIEL BOURNE: Let me ask you about your past, then, your influences and so on.

BORGES: Well, I can tell you about the influences I have received, but not about the influence I may have had upon others. That's quite unknown to me and I don't care about it. But I think of myself primarily as a reader, then also a writer, but that's more or less irrelevant. I think I'm a good reader, I'm a good reader in many languages, especially in English, since poetry came to me through the English language, initially through my father's love of Swinburne, of Tennyson, and also of Keats, Shelley and so on—not through my native tongue, not through Spanish. It came to me as a kind of spell. I didn't understand it, but I felt it. My father gave me the free run of his library. When I think of my boyhood, I think in terms of the books I read.

BOURNE: You are indeed a bookman. Can you give us a notion of how your librarianship and antiquarian tastes have helped your writings in terms of freshness?

BORGES: I wonder if my writing has any freshness. I think of myself as belonging essentially to the nineteenth century. I was born in the last but one year of the century, 1899, and also my reading has been confined—well, I also read contemporary writers—but I was brought up on Dickens and the Bible, or Mark Twain. Of course I am interested in the past. Perhaps one of the reasons is we cannot make, cannot change the past. I mean you can hardly unmake the present. But the past, after all, is merely to say a memory, a dream. You know my own past seems continually changed when I am remembering it, or reading things that are interesting to me. I think that I owe much to many writers, perhaps to the writers I have read or who were really part of their language, a part of tradition. A language in itself is a tradition.

STEPHEN CAPE: If we could, let's turn to your poetry.

BORGES: My friends tell me that I am an intruder, that I don't really write when I attempt poetry. But those of my friends who write in prose say that I'm no writer when I attempt prose. So really I don't know what to do, I'm in a quandary.

CAPE: One modern poet, Gary Snyder, describes his poetic theory in a short poem called "Riprap."[2] His ideas seem to have some things in common with your poetry, and I'd like to quote a short section of it which describes his attitudes towards words in poems.

2   SC reads Gary Snyder's "Riprap," from *Riprap*. San Francisco: Origen Press, 1959.

BORGES: Yes but why a short section, a large section would be better, no? I want to enjoy this morning.

CAPE: The title "Riprap" refers to making a path of stones on slippery rock, to get pack horses up a mountain, a small inter-connected path.

BORGES: Of course, he writes with varied metaphors, and I don't, I write in a simple way. But he has the English language to play with, and I haven't.

CAPE: His idea seems to be comparing placing words in a poem with building the inter-connected trail where each piece is dependent on the piece on either side. Do you agree with that type of approach towards the structure of a poem, or is it just one of many?

BORGES: Well, I think as Kipling said, "There are nine and sixty ways of constructing tribal lays, / and-every-single-one-of-them-is-right"—and that may be one of the right ways. But mine is not at all like that. I get—it's some kind of rela-tion, a rather dim one. I'm given an idea; well, that idea may become a tale or a poem. But I'm only given the starting point and the goal. And then I have to invent or concoct somehow what happens in between, and then I do my best. But gen-erally, when I get that kind of inspiration, I do all I can to resist it, but if it keeps bothering me, then I have to somehow write it down. But I never look for subjects. They come to me in a cage, they may come when I'm trying to sleep, or when I wake up. They come to me on the streets of Buenos Aires, or anywhere at anytime. For example, a week ago I had a dream. When I awoke—it was a nightmare—I said, well, this nightmare isn't worth telling, but I think there's a story lurking here. I want to find it. Now when I think I found it, I write it within five or six months. I take my time over it. So I have, let's say, a different method. Every craftsman has his own method, of course, and I should respect it.

CAPE: Snyder's trying to achieve a direct transfer of his state of mind to the reader with as little interference as possible from reasoning. He's going for the direct transfer of sensation. Does this seem a little extreme for you?

BORGES: No, but he seems to be a very cautious poet. Where I'm really old and innocent. I just ramble on, try to find my way. People tell me, for example, what message I have. I'm afraid I haven't any. Well, here's fable, what's the moral? I'm afraid I don't know. I'm merely a dreamer, and then a writer, and my happiest moments are when I'm a reader.

CAPE: Do you think of words as having effects that are inherent in the word or in the images they carry?

BORGES: Well, yes, for example, if you attempt a sonnet, then, at least in Spanish, you have to use certain words. There's only a few rhymes. And those of course may be used as metaphors, peculiar metaphors, since you have to stick to them. I would even venture to say—this of course is a sweeping statement—but perhaps the word *moon* in English stems from something different than the word *luna* in Latin or Spanish. The *moon*, the word *moon*, is a lingering sound. *Moon* is a beautiful word. The French word is also beautiful: *lune*. But in Old English the word was *mona*. The word isn't beautiful at all, two syllables. And then the Greek is worse. We have *celena*, three syllables. But the word *moon* is a beautiful word. That sound is not found, let's say in Spanish. *The moon*. I can linger in words. Words inspire you. Words have a life of their own.

CAPE: The word's life of its own, does that seem more important than the meaning that it gives in a particular context?

BORGES: I think that the meanings are more or less irrelevant. What is important, or the two important facts I should say, are emotion, and then words arising from emotion. I don't think you can write in an emotionless way. If you attempt it, the result is artificial. I don't like that kind of writing. I think that if a poem is really great, you should think of it as having written itself despite the author. It should flow.

CAPE: Could one set of myths be replaced by another when moving from one poet to another and still get the same poetic effect?

BORGES: I suppose every poet has his own private mythology. Maybe he's unaware of it. People tell me that I have evolved a private mythology of tigers, of blades, of labyrinths, and I'm unaware of the fact this is so. My readers are finding it all the time. But I think perhaps that is the duty of a poet. When I think of America, I always tend to think in terms of Walt Whitman. The word *Manhattan* was invented for him, no?

CAPE: An image of a healthy America?

BORGES: Well, yes. At the same time, Walt Whitman himself was a myth, a myth of a man who wrote, a very unfortunate man, very lonely, and yet he made of himself a rather splendid vagabond. I have pointed out that Whitman is perhaps the only writer on earth who has managed to create a mythological person of himself and one of the three persons of the Trinity is the reader, because when you read Walt Whitman, you are Walt Whitman. Very strange that he did that, the only person on earth. Of course, America has produced writers important all over the world. Especially New England. You have given the world men that cannot be thought away. For example, all contemporary literature could not be what it is had it not been for Poe, for Whitman, and perhaps Melville and Henry James. But South America, we have many things important to us and Spain, but not to the rest of the world. I do think that Spanish literature began by being very fine. And then somewhere, and already with such writers as Quevado and Gongora, you feel something has stiffened; the language doesn't flow as it did.

BOURNE: Does this hold for the twentieth century? There's Lorca, for example.

BORGES: But I'm not fond of Lorca. Well, you see, this is a shortcoming of mine, I dislike visual poetry. He is visual all the time, and he goes in for fancy metaphors. But, of course, I know he's very respected. I knew him personally. He lived a year in New York. He didn't learn a word of English after a year in New York. Very strange. I met him only once in Buenos Aires. And then, it was a lucky thing for him to be executed. Best thing to happen for a poet. A fine death, no? An impressive death. And then Antonio Machado wrote that beautiful poem about him.

CAPE: The Hopi Indians are used as an example many times, because of the nature of their language, of how language and vocabulary thought—

BORGES: I know very little about it. I was told of the Pampas Indians by my grandmother. She lived all of her life in Junín; that was on the western end of civilization. She told me as a fact that their arithmetic went thus. She held up a hand and said, "I'll teach you the Pampas Indians' mathematics." "I won't understand." "Yes," she said, "you will. Look at my hands: one, two, three, four, many." So, infinity went on her thumb. I have noticed, in what literary men call the *Pampas*, that the people have but little notion of distance. They don't think in terms of miles, of leagues.

BOURNE: A friend of mine who comes from Kentucky tells me that they talk of distance there as one mountain, two mountains away.

BORGES: Oh, really? How strange.

CAPE: Does changing from Spanish to English to German or Old English seem to offer you different means of viewing the world?

BORGES: I don't think languages are essentially synonymous. In Spanish it is very difficult to make things flow, because words are over-long. But in English, you have light words. For example, if you say *slowly, quickly*, in English, what you hear is the meaningful part of the word: *slow-ly, quick-ly*. You hear *slow* and *quick*. But in Spanish you say *lentamente, rápidamente*, and what you hear is the *-mente*. That is gratis, so to say. A friend of mine translated Shakespeare's sonnets into Spanish. I said that he needed two Spanish sonnets to a single English one, since English words are short and to the point, but Spanish words are over-long. And English also has a physical quality to it. Well, in English, you can say: *to explain away*. In Kipling's "The Ballad of East and West," an English officer is pursuing an Afghan horse thief. They're both on horseback. And Kipling writes: "They have ridden the low moon out of the sky. / Their hooves drum up the dawn." Now you can't *ride the low moon out of the sky* in Spanish, and you can't *drum up the dawn*. It can't be done. Even such simple sentences as *he fell down* or *he picked himself up*, you can't do in Spanish. You have to say *he got up the best he could* or some lame paraphrase. But in English you can do much with verbs and positions. You can write: *dream away your life; live up to; something you have to live down*. Those things are impossible in Spanish. They cannot be done. Then you have compound words. For example you have *wordsmith*. It would be in Spanish *un herrero de palabras*, rather stilted, rather uncouth. But it can be done in German, you can make up words all the time, but not in English. You are not allowed the freedom that the Anglo-Saxons had. For example, you have *sigefolc*, or *victorious people*. Now in Old English, you don't think of these words as being artificial, but in Spanish it can't be done. But of course, you have what I think is beautiful in Spanish: the sounds are very clear. But in English you have lost your open vowels.

CAPE: What was it that attracted you to Anglo-Saxon poetry originally?

BORGES: Well, I lost my eyesight for reading purposes when I was made chief librarian for the Argentine National Library. I said, I won't bow down and allow self-pity. I will attempt something else. And then, I remember, I had at home *Sweet's Anglo-Saxon Reader* and *The Anglo-Saxon Chronicles*. And I said, We'll attempt Anglo-Saxon. And then I began; I studied through *Sweet's Anglo-Saxon Reader*. And then I fell in love with it through two words. Those two words, I can still recall them, those words were the name of London, *Lundenburh*; and then Rome, *Romeburh*. And now I'm attempting Old Norse, which was a finer literature than Old English.

CAPE: How would you describe a twentieth-century mythology for writers?

BOURNE: That's a big question!

BORGES: I don't think it should be done consciously. You don't have to try to be contemporary. You are already contemporary. What one has in mythology is being evolved all the time. Personally, I think I can do with Greek and Old Norse mythology. For example, I don't think I stand in need of planes or of railways or of cars.

CHARLES SILVER: I wondered if there were any particular mystical or religious readings you've done that have influenced you?

BORGES: Yes, I have done some reading, of course, in English and in German, of the Sufis. And then, I think, before I die, I'll do my best to write a book on Swedenborg the mystic. And Blake also was a mystic. But I dislike Blake's mythology. It seems very artificial.

BOURNE: You said, "When one reads Whitman, one is Whitman," and I was wondering, when you translated Kafka did you feel at any time that you were Kafka in any sense?

BORGES: Well, I felt that I owed so much to Kafka that I really didn't need to exist. But, really, I am merely a word for Chesterton, for Kafka, and Sir Thomas Browne—I love him. I translated him into seventeenth-century Spanish and it worked very well. We took a chapter out of *Urne Buriall* and we did that into Quevado's Spanish and it went very well—the same period, the same idea of writing Latin in a different language, writing Latin in English, writing Latin in Spanish.

BOURNE: You were the first to translate Kafka into Spanish. Did you feel a sense of mission while you were translating him?

BORGES: No, that was when I translated Walt Whitman's *Song of Myself*. "What I'm doing is very important," I said to myself. Of course I know Whitman by heart.

BOURNE: Did you feel that in any of your translations that by doing them you'd help the understanding and appreciation of your own work, did they ever seem to justify what you yourself had done?

BORGES: No, I never think of my own work . . .

BOURNE: When you translate . . .

BORGES: No, at home, come visit in Buenos Aires, I'll show you my library, you won't find a single book of mine. I'm very sure of this—I choose my books. Who am I to find my way into the neighborhood of Sir Thomas Browne, or of Emerson. I'm nobody.

BOURNE: So Borges the writer and Borges the translator are completely separate?

BORGES: Yes, they are. When I translate, I try not to intrude. I try to do a fair translation of some kind, and to be a poet also.

BOURNE: You said that you don't ever try to put any meaning into your works.

BORGES: Well, you see, I think of myself as being an ethical man, but I don't try to teach ethics. I have no message. I know little about contemporary life. I don't read a newspaper. I dislike politics and politicians. I belong to no party whatever. My private life is a private life. I try to avoid photography and publicity. My father had the same idea. He said to me, "I want to be Wells's Invisible Man." He was quite proud of it. In Rio de Janeiro, there, nobody knew my name. I did feel invisible there. And somehow, publicity has found me. What can I do about it? I don't look for it. It has found me. Of course, one lives to be eighty, one is found out, one is detected.

BOURNE: About meaning in your work or the absence of meaning in it—in Kafka's work there is guilt running all the way through, and in your writing everything's beyond guilt.

BORGES: Yes, that's true. Kafka had the sense of guilt. I don't think I have because I don't believe in free will. Because what I have done has been done, well, for me or through me. But I haven't done it really. But I don't believe in free will, I can't feel guilty.

BOURNE: Could this be tied in then with you saying that there is only a finite combination of elements and so actually the conception of ideas is only a rediscovery of the past?

BORGES: Yes, I suppose it is. I suppose that each generation has to rewrite the books of the past and do it in a slightly different way. When I write a poem, that one has already been written down any amount of times, but I have to rediscover it. That's my moral duty. I suppose we all attempt very slight variations, but the language itself can hardly be changed. Joyce, of course, tried to do it. But he failed, though he wrote some beautiful lines.

BOURNE: Would you say then that all of these poems that have been rewritten are the coming back upon the same wall in the labyrinth?

BORGES: Yes, I would. That's a good metaphor, yes. Of course it would be.

BOURNE: Can you give us some guidelines as to when you think using local color is legitimate and when it is not?

BORGES: I think, if you can do it in an unobtrusive way, it is all for the good. But if you stress it, the whole thing is artificial. But it should be used, I mean, it's not forbidden. But you don't have to stress it. We have evolved a kind of slang in Buenos Aires. Writers are, well, abusing it, over-using it. But the people themselves have little use for it. They may say a word in slang every twenty minutes or so, but nobody tries to talk slang all the time.

BOURNE: Are there any North American writers that you felt conveyed this local color to you effectively as an outsider to that culture?

BORGES: Yes, I think that Mark Twain gave me a lot. And then, I wonder if Ring Lardner gave me something else also. You think of him as being very, very American, no?

BOURNE: And urban . . .

BORGES: More urban, yes. And then, what other writers? Of course, I have read Bret Harte. I think that Faulkner was a very great writer—I dislike Hemingway, by the way—but Faulkner was a great writer, despite, well, telling a story the wrong way and mixing up the chronology.

BOURNE: You translated Faulkner's *Wild Palms.*

BORGES: Yes, but I'm not too fond of that book. I think that *Light in August* is far better. And that book that he despised, *Sanctuary*, is a very striking book also. That was the first Faulkner I read, and went onto others. I read his poetry also.

BOURNE: When you were translating Faulkner and his use

of local color, how did you deal with it, did you stick with
straight Spanish or did you try to put it into a type of local
Spanish?

BORGES: No, I think that if one has to translate slang one
should translate it into straight Spanish, because you're not . . .
you get a different kind of local color. For example, we have
a translation of a poem of ours called "El gaucho, Martín
Fierro." Now, it has been done into cowboy English. That is
wrong, I should say, because you think of cowboys and not
of gauchos. I would translate "Martín Fierro," into as pure an
English as I could get. Because though the cowboy and the
gaucho may be the same type of man, you think of them in
a different way. For example, when you think of a cowboy,
well, you think of guns. But when you think of a gaucho, you
think of daggers and duels. The whole thing is done in a very
different way. I have seen some of it. I have seen an old man,
of seventy-five or so, challenge a young man to a duel, and he
said, "I'll be back in no time." He came back with two very
dangerous-looking daggers, one of them with a silver hilt,
and one larger than the other. They were not the same size.
He put them on the table and said, "Well, now, choose your
weapon." So you see, when he said that, he was using a kind
of rhetoric. He meant: "You can choose the larger one, I don't
mind." And then the younger man of course apologized. The
old man had many daggers in his house, but he chose those
two on purpose. Those two daggers said, "This old man knows
how to handle a dagger, since he can choose the other one."

BOURNE: That brings to mind your stories . . .

BORGES: Well, of course, I've used them for my stories; from telling a person's experience, comes stories afterward, of course.

BOURNE: There's meaning in there, but you don't have to mention the meaning, you just have to tell what happened.

BORGES: Well, the meaning is that the man was a hoodlum; he was a sharper. But at the same time he had a code of honor. I mean he would not think of attacking someone without fair warning. I mean he knew the way that those things were done. The whole thing was done very, very slowly. A man might begin by praising another. Then you would want to say that where he came from nobody knew how to fight. You might teach him, perhaps. Then after that, he would interrupt the other with words of praise, and then after that he would say, "Let us walk into the street," "Choose your weapon," and so on. But this whole thing was done very slowly, very gently. I wonder if that kind of rhetoric has been lost. I suppose it has. Well, they use firearms now, revolvers, and all that code has disappeared. You can shoot a man from a distance.

BOURNE: Knife-fighting is more intimate.

BORGES: It is intimate, yes. Well, I used that word. At the end of a poem I used that word. A man is having his throat cut and then I say, "the intimate end of knife on his throat."

BOURNE: You said new writers should begin by imitating old forms and established writers.

BORGES: I think it's a question of honesty, no? If you want to renew something you must show that you can do what has been done. You can't begin by innovation. You can't begin by free verse for example. You should attempt a sonnet, or any other set stanza, and then go on to the new things.

BOURNE: When is the time to break away? Can you give some idea from your own experience when you knew it was time to go into a new approach?

BORGES: No, because I made the mistake. I began by free verse. I did not know how to handle it. Very difficult, and then, I found out that, after all, writing with free verse you have to make your own pattern and change it all the time. Well, prose, prose comes after the poetry of course. Prose is more difficult. I don't know. I have written by instinct. I don't think I'm a very conscious poet.

BOURNE: You said that someone should begin with the more or less traditional forms. Isn't it though a matter of audience?

BORGES: No, I never thought of an audience. When I printed my first book I didn't send it to the bookshops, or to other writers, just gave copies away to friends—some three hundred copies I gave away to friends. They were not on sale. But of course, in those days nobody thought about a writer being famous, or failure or success. Those ideas were alien to us around 1920, 1930. Nobody thought in terms of failure or success in selling books. We thought of writing as, I would say as a pastime, or as a kind of destiny. And when I read De Quincey's *Autobiography*, I found out that he always knew that his life would be a literary life, and Milton also, and Coleridge also, I think. They knew it all the time. They knew their lives would be given over to literature, for reading and for writing, which, of course, go together.

BOURNE: Your short prose piece "Borges and I" and the poem "The Watcher" show your fascination with the Double. Could we let Borges the non-writer speak for a while and give some sort of assessment of the writer Borges's work, whether he likes it or not?

BORGES: I don't like it too much. I prefer original texts. I prefer Chesterton and Kafka.

BOURNE: So do you think it's the non-writer's decision that your library in Argentina doesn't have any of Borges's books?

BORGES: Yes, of course.

BOURNE: He made himself felt in that situation.

BORGES: Yes, he did, yes. You won't find a single book of his around me, because I warned him I'm sick and tired. I warned him of the way I feel. I say, well, here's Borges back again.

What can I do?—put up with him. Everyone feels that way I suppose.

BOURNE: A comment that Jean-Paul Sartre made has always fascinated me. He said: "Man is a wizard unto man." What do you think about that? Would you agree?

BORGES: Man is a wizard?

BOURNE: He concocts ideas, he concocts laws of the universe, and tries to make his fellow man believe them. Would you agree with that?

BORGES: I suppose that would be applied especially to poets and to writers, no? And to theologians of course. After all, if you think of the Trinity, it's far stranger than Edgar Allan Poe. The Father, the Son and the Holy Ghost, and they're boiled down into one single Being. Very, very strange. But nobody believes in it, supposedly. At least I don't.

BOURNE: Myths don't have to believed to be effective, though.

BORGES: No, and yet, I wonder. For example, our imagination accepts a centaur, but not, let's say, a bull with the face of a cat. No. That would be no good, very, very uncouth. But you accept the Minotaur, the centaur, because they are beautiful. Well, at least we think of them as being beautiful. They of course are a part of tradition. But Dante, who had never seen monuments, had never seen coins, he knew the Greek myths through Latin writers. And he thought of the Minotaur as being a bull with a human bearded face. Very ugly. In the many editions of Dante you see that kind of Minotaur, while you think of him as a man with the face of a bull. But since Dante had read *semi-boven, semi-hominem,* he thought of him in that way. And our imagination can hardly accept that idea. But as I think of the many myths, there is one that is very harmful, and that is the myth of countries. I mean, why should I think of myself as being an Argentine, and not a Chilean, and not an Uruguayan. I don't know really. All of those myths that we impose on ourselves—and they make for hatred, for war, for enmity—are very harmful. Well, I suppose in the long run, governments and countries will die out and we'll be just, well, cosmopolitans.

THE LAST INTERVIEW

INTERVIEW BY GLORIA LÓPEZ LECUBE

LA ISLA RADIO FM RADIO, ARGENTINA, 1985

TRANSLATED BY KIT MAUDE

GLORIA LÓPEZ LECUBE: In addition to writing and having your favorite books read to you, what do you feel compelled to do?

BORGES: I like to travel, I like to get a feeling for countries, and imagine them; very probably inaccurately because . . .

LÓPEZ LECUBE: So your companion describes them to you?

BORGES: Yes, I travel with María Kodama, she describes things to me and I imagine them, poorly of course.

LÓPEZ LECUBE: Do you imagine them in color?

BORGES: Yes, usually, and I dream in color too, but when I dream in color the colors are too dazzling. In my waking hours, however, right now for instance, I'm surrounded by a fog, it's bright, sometimes bluish, sometimes gray, and the shapes aren't very well defined. The last color to stay with me was yellow. I wrote a book, *The Gold of the Tigers*, and in that book—it was a poem—I said, quite accurately I think, that the first color I ever saw was the yellow of a tiger's fur. I used to spend hours and hours staring at the tigers at the zoo, and when I began to lose my sight the only color left to me was yellow, but now I've lost that too. The first colors I lost were black and red, which means that I am never in darkness. At first this was a little uncomfortable. Then I was left with the other colors; green, blue and yellow, but green and blue faded into brown and then the yellow disappeared. Now no colors are left, just light and movement.

LÓPEZ LECUBE: You once said that blindness was a gift bestowed upon you so that people would like you.

BORGES: Well, that's how I try to think, but believe me . . .

LÓPEZ LECUBE: It didn't make you angry?

BORGES: Believe me: the benefits of blindness have been greatly exaggerated. If I could see, I would never leave the house, I'd stay indoors reading the many books that surround me. Now they're as far away from me as Iceland, although I've been to Iceland twice and I will never reach my books. And yet, at the same time, the fact that I can't read obliges me . . .

LÓPEZ LECUBE: To connect with the world?

BORGES: No, not to connect with the world, no. It obliges me to dream and imagine. No, I get to know the world mainly through people.

LÓPEZ LECUBE: But it doesn't make you angry? Doesn't being blind make you feel impotent?

BORGES: No, well, privately it can, but my duty is to ...

LÓPEZ LECUBE: When precisely do you feel that *bronca*[3]?

BORGES: No, *bronca* is too strong a word.

LÓPEZ LECUBE: You never feel *bronca*?

BORGES: I don't know, *bronca* is *lunfardo*[4] for anger isn't it? I don't know, no, not anger, sometimes I feel deflated, but that's natural, and at my age ... old age is a form of deflation too, but why be angry about it? It's no one's fault.

LÓPEZ LECUBE: Do you remember what your face, body or hands look like?

BORGES: No.

LÓPEZ LECUBE: Do you touch your face? With your hands?

BORGES: Well, of course, before or after shaving, but not much. Who knows what sort of old man is watching me through the mirror? I can't see him, of course. I probably wouldn't recognize him in the mirror (which I no longer have, of course); the last time I saw myself was around 1957. I fear that I've changed greatly; it's a wrinkled landscape, no doubt.

3 A slang word for "frustration" or "anger."
4 Buenos Aires slang invented primarily by tango writers and singers in Buenos Aires in the first half of the twentieth century.

LÓPEZ LECUBE: But wrinkles are also a sign of experience.

BORGES: Yes, for example, I used to have chestnut hair and now I suspect that I'm beyond baldness. [*Laughs.*]

LÓPEZ LECUBE: You have plenty of hair, you can't complain.

BORGES: Yes, but it's strange to be bald and have your hair messed up at the same time.

LÓPEZ LECUBE: You're blind and yet when I speak to you I feel as though you're looking at me, why would that be?

BORGES: Well, it's a trick. As you describe it, it sounds like a facial lie.

LÓPEZ LECUBE: By me or you?

BORGES: No, as your voice is coming from over there, I have to look over there, and then you feel as though I'm looking at you. If you like, I can close my eyes, if that would make you feel more comfortable, I can't tell the difference.

LÓPEZ LECUBE: No, I feel as though we were looking at each other.

BORGES: Well, if only that were true. Or maybe we are looking at each other; I think that our senses only detect so much.

LÓPEZ LECUBE: What do you feel when you're walking down

the street? Because you're a kind of thermometer aren't you? An aural thermometer, out among the people?

BORGES: I feel surrounded by friendship; generous, inexplicable friendship. People like me, I don't know why. I can't explain it; most people haven't read what I've written. These friendships are mysterious but in a marvelous way, as though I were a relic. When I went to Texas, in '61, with my mother, I found it strange that people took me seriously, I asked myself why that would be. I think that I've hit upon the answer; I thought, "Of course!" I was sixty-two, and people say that's old, I don't think I was really; to me I was young, but other people thought that I was. So, I was an old man, sixty-one years old, I was a poet, I was blind, and this made me something like a Milton, something like a Homer. And of course I was South American, which is exotic in Texas, to them I was a sort of Mexican, and these were all strong cards in my hand, cards in my favor, apart from what I'd written, which hadn't yet been translated. So I felt confident in the fact that I was an old, blind, South American poet, but in Buenos Aires I hadn't yet been noticed; they were very, very snobbish in Buenos Aires and only noticed me when they found out that I had been given a prize, the Formentor Prize, by European editors. So suddenly, they noticed that I was there. Up until then I had been Wells's Invisible Man, which was more comfortable, but all of a sudden they started to pay attention to me.

LÓPEZ LECUBE: And what happened when they started to pay more attention to you? Especially given your characteristic shyness?

BORGES: My shyness has actually grown more acute over time, just like my terror of speaking in public: I was less afraid the first time than I am now because I'm a veteran, let's say, of the panic.

LÓPEZ LECUBE: Panic? How do you feel when you're standing in front of an audience?

BORGES: Now, I'm terrified, but of course my blindness can be a defense: my friends will tell me that no one's come, that the hall is empty, but I know they say this to ease my nerves. Then, sometimes, I'll go out into the hall, hear the applause and realize that my friends have, generously, been lying to me and I start to feel that depression again.

LÓPEZ LECUBE: But you speak so easily . . .

BORGES: No, no, no, believe me, it's so difficult, I find writing for myself especially difficult.

LÓPEZ LECUBE: How many canes do you have, Borges?

BORGES: Seven or eight; they're quite rustic.

LÓPEZ LECUBE: Are they gifts?

BORGES: Yes, they're gifts.

LÓPEZ LECUBE: From people in the countries you visit or . . . ?

BORGES: Well, some of them, and the rest are from María Kodama, they're Arab shepherd's crooks from nearby Canaan.

LÓPEZ LECUBE: And do you always dress like that, in a suit and tie?

BORGES: Yes, but I don't know what color this suit is, because I'm blind.

LÓPEZ LECUBE: Mmmm ... I'm not going to tell you.

BORGES: You could tell me that it's a harlequin costume and I could decide whether to believe you or not, but let's hope not.

LÓPEZ LECUBE: Actually it's a bright red suit with a pink shirt and a pink tie ...

BORGES: Really? A pink shirt? Isn't that a little daring? I didn't ... I thought it was a white shirt.

LÓPEZ LECUBE: No, it's not true, I'm joking; you're dressed perfectly.

BORGES: Yes, I don't think we have any pink shirts at home, I wouldn't have allowed it.

LÓPEZ LECUBE: No, the shirt is beige, the suit is light brown and you're wearing a beautiful Yves Saint Laurent beige and violet tie.

BORGES: Oh good, it sounded a little strange to me, but that's fine.

LÓPEZ LECUBE: Don't worry.

BORGES: Violet?

LÓPEZ LECUBE: It's lovely.

BORGES: How strange, I don't like violet, but if the color looks good, I'm not ... [*Laughs.*]

LÓPEZ LECUBE: Who dresses you, Fanny?

BORGES: No, María Kodama.

LÓPEZ LECUBE: Oh, because you have a maid, a *salteña*⁵ woman, at home ...

BORGES: Nooo ...

LÓPEZ LECUBE: ... who speaks to us journalists and says "The señor is sleeping" or "He's sleeping."

BORGES: That "salteña" is actually correntina.⁶

LÓPEZ LECUBE: Oh, I'm sorry, I thought she was from Salta.

5 Salta is a province in northern Argentina.
6 From Corrientes, another province in Argentina.

BORGES: She's from the province and speaks Guaraní, but I don't understand a word of it . . .

LÓPEZ LECUBE: Borges, how do you imagine your death?

BORGES: Ah, I'm waiting for it very impatiently, I'm told that it will come but I feel as though it won't, that I'm not going to die. Spinoza says that we all feel immortal, yes, but not as individuals, I assume, rather immortal in a pantheist way, in a divine way. When I get scared, when things aren't going so well, I think to myself, "But why should I care what happens to a South American writer, from a lost country like the Republic of Argentina at the end of the twentieth century? What possible interest could that hold for me when I still have the adventure of death before me, which could be annihilation; that would be best, it could be oblivion . . ."

LÓPEZ LECUBE: Or it could be the start of an adventure . . .

BORGES: It could be, but I hope not. I hope it's the end. You're a pessimist. I was thinking about a story about precisely this, concerning a man who spends his whole life waiting hopefully to die and then it turns out that he continues living and he's extremely disappointed. Eventually, however, he gets accustomed to his posthumous life, just as he got used to the previous one, which is invariably hard.

I don't think that a day passes when we're not both very happy and very unhappy, in that sense we're like Joyce's *Ulysses*.

Ulysses, of course, takes place over twenty-four hours and over these twenty-four hours, everything that happened to Ulysses on his return to Ithaca occurs. That's what the title *Ulysses* means. Read it because all of time fits inside that tunnel, that odyssey, and this is what happens to us every day. And at the moment, well, I feel quite happy talking to you, and it seems strange to me that what I'm saying is being recorded; the fact that people take me seriously is what surprises me the most. I don't take myself seriously, but people do . . .

LÓPEZ LECUBE: To me, this image, this humility . . .

BORGES: No, no, it's not humility, its lucidity. It's not humility, I hate humility. I find false modesty horrible.

LÓPEZ LECUBE: You once said that you'd rather be someone else, not Jorge Luis Borges . . .

BORGES: Yes, that phrase is plagiarized; I found it in a book by Papini I read when I was young. It's called *El piloto ciego* and says that he wanted to be someone else and of course he thinks that he's the only one who wants to be someone else, but we all want to be other people.

LÓPEZ LECUBE: And you? Who do you want to be?

BORGES: [*Pause.*] No, I have to resign myself to being Borges, I can't imagine any other destiny for myself.

LÓPEZ LECUBE: You can't imagine being someone else?

BORGES: No, no. Or in another century either.

LÓPEZ LECUBE: In another country?

BORGES: In another country, yes. I've lived in Switzerland, I'd like to die in Switzerland, why not? I'm an alumnus of Geneva, my only degree is a baccalaureate from my school in Geneva, all the others are honorary; I was given those.

LÓPEZ LECUBE: And what profession in Switzerland?

BORGES: My only destiny is literary. I read a biography of Milton and another of Coleridge. It seems that they knew they were going to be writers right from the beginning.

LÓPEZ LECUBE: And when did you realize that?

BORGES: I think I have always known. Maybe because my father had an influence on me; I was raised in my father's library, I went to school, but that hardly matters don't you think? I was really raised in my father's library. I always knew that that would be my destiny, being among books, reading them, but it would seem that I was influenced to write as well.

LÓPEZ LECUBE: Have you ever tried to paint?

BORGES: No, not that I can remember. I'm very clumsy. I couldn't.

LÓPEZ LECUBE: You don't know how to do anything other than write?

BORGES: Well, at one point I knew how to swim, to ride a horse, use my body. Ride a bicycle [*laughs*] like everyone else. Apparently the height of aspiration in China right now is to own a wristwatch and a bicycle.

LÓPEZ LECUBE: Which of your poems do you like the most? And why? The ones you remember as being most definitely yours? The ones in which you express yourself the most?

BORGES: No, I don't like the ones about me. There's a sonnet about Spinoza that I like. I wrote two sonnets about him: in one of them, a line I remember says "Someone ..." no. "A man creates God in the darkness,"[7] that man is Spinoza who engenders God, his God, made of an infinite substance whose tributes will be infinite. And I also wrote another sonnet about Spinoza. I remember two sonnets about me; one of them about the death of my grandfather Colonel Borges soon after Mitre's surrender at La Verde.[8] My grandfather killed

7 Borges says "tiniebla" while the poem actually reads "penumbra."
8 In 1874, Bartolomé Mitre, a prominent liberal general and politician, led a short-lived revolution that ended with defeat in the battle of La Verde and surrender of his army on December 3, 1874.

himself after Mitre's surrender. In 1874, the year my father was born, and Lugones,[9] too; 1874–1938 . . .

LÓPEZ LECUBE: What a coincidence . . .

BORGES: Except that Lugones decided that he wanted to die; Lugones killed himself on an island in Tigre, as I'm sure you've been told. My father, well, my father had a hemiplegia, which was apparently incurable, and he said to me: "I'm not going to ask you to put a bullet through my head because you won't do it, but I'll manage." Effectively, he refused to eat, except when he had a burning thirst and drank water. He refused all medication, didn't let them give him injections, and after a few months he managed to die. So my father's death was a kind of suicide too, but one that involved more suffering because my grandfather just advanced onto a line of rifles and well, two bullets from a Remington . . . My father, on the other hand had to wait several months refusing all food. The second form of suicide must have required more bravery.

LÓPEZ LECUBE: I get the feeling that you're a kind of saint who doesn't recognize his literary worth, saying that you've been given prizes for insignificant work . . .

BORGES: Yes, that's true . . .

LÓPEZ LECUBE: But really you're more . . .

9   Leopoldo Lugones (1874–1938), Argentine poet.

BORGES: I'd like to be a saint, why not? [*Laughs.*] Why reject sainthood? I've tried to be an analytical man, which is enough isn't it? No, I'm not a saint.

LÓPEZ LECUBE: But really . . .

BORGES: But actually, why not? If you see me as a saint right now, I have no problem with being a saint.

LÓPEZ LECUBE: For everything you've done for Argentine literature?

BORGES: Well, no, because that's been minimal. I haven't influenced anyone, and yet in contrast I owe so much to so many writers from the past.

LÓPEZ LECUBE: But how is it that you think you haven't had any influence?

BORGES: No, I owe much to Groussac,[10] I owe much to Lugones, I owe much to Capdevila,[11] I owe much to Fernández Moreno,[12] without a doubt. Almafuerte,[13] I don't know if I'm worthy of him. The only man of genius Argentina has

10 Paul-François Groussac (1848–1929), Franco-Argentine writer, historian and literary critic.
11 Arturo Capdevila (1889–1967), Argentine poet and writer.
12 Baldomero Fernández Moreno (1886–1950), Argentine poet.
13 The pen name of Pedro Bonifacio Palacios (1854–1917), Argentine poet and doctor.

produced is Almafuerte, the author of "El misionero," Carriego could recite "El misionero" from memory. My first contact with pure literature was one Sunday night with Carriego, who was an unremarkable-looking man, at home, standing and reciting "El misionero" in quite a booming voice. I didn't understand a word, but I felt that I had discovered something new, and that new thing was poetry.

LÓPEZ LECUBE: The power . . .

BORGES: Yes, it came to me from Almafuerte, but through Carriego who recited him very well. I remember: "*Yo deliré de hambre muchos días y no dormí de frío muchas noches, / para salvar a Dios de los reproches de su hambruna humana y sus noches frías.*"[14] That's from the end of "El misionero."

LÓPEZ LECUBE: If we were in your library right now, what poem would you ask me to read to you?

BORGES: The poem "Acquainted with the Night" by Robert Frost, or we could open the book *La fiesta del mundo* by Arturo Capdevila. I'd tell you to open it anywhere and just start reading to surprise me. Especially the poem "Aulo Gelio" which has some admirable verses that no one remembers any more: "*(Si los Lacedemonios al combate, iban a son de lira o son de flauta, ¿en cuántas drachmas cotizó Corinto? La noche de la*

14 "I was driven delirious with hunger for many days and many nights I couldn't sleep for the cold / to defend God from reproach for human hunger and his cold nights."

Laís la cortesana),"[15] that's by Capdevila, it's admirable. And yet it seems that he's been forgotten because people tend to forget easily, or they remember stupid things like a football match, for example, or the founding fathers. I'm a descendent of the founding fathers, but I don't know if they're worth much thought. We have a history, but I don't know if it's filled with men of ideas, equestrian social strata, rather.

LÓPEZ LECUBE: Why shouldn't you be described as a genius?

BORGES: There's no reason why I should be. What have I written? Transcriptions of writing by other people.

LÓPEZ LECUBE: But it's not just what you've written, it's how you've exposed the Argentine being, describing what's happening . . .

BORGES: No, not at all, I haven't done anything . . .

LÓPEZ LECUBE: How you got involved with political events, how you spoke out about the military dictatorship.

BORGES: Well, because I was getting such sad news, and also

15 The verse actually reads: "*(Si los lacedemonios al combate iban a son de trompa o son de flauta / si en diez mil dracmas cotizó Corinto la noche de Lais, la cortesana.)*" "(If the Laconians sallied forth into combat to the rhythm of the horn or the flute / if Lais, the courtesan, priced Corinth at ten thousand drachmas.)"

I knew that I was in a fairly untouchable position. I could speak out against the military, against the war, without being in any danger.

LÓPEZ LECUBE: And you did.

BORGES: And I did.

LÓPEZ LECUBE: Another person might not have.

BORGES: But it was my duty, I did it for ethical reasons. I haven't read a newspaper in my life; news reaches me indirectly but surely. For example the Mothers and Grandmothers of the Plaza de Mayo[16] came to my house, maybe their children were terrorists, maybe they got what they deserved, but the tears of those women were sincere, they weren't acting, they weren't hysterical, and I saw this, and so I spoke out. It was my duty, many others did too . . . yes.

LÓPEZ LECUBE: Do you lie, Borges?

BORGES: Not voluntarily. But I can lie, language is so limited compared to what we think and feel that we are obliged to lie, words themselves are lies. Stevenson said that in five minutes of any man's life things happen that all of Shakespeare's vocabulary and talents would be unable to describe adequately.

16 Human rights groups who campaigned for the release of political prisoners and the end to torture and killings during the dictatorship.

Language is a clumsy tool and that can oblige one to lie. Lie deliberately? No. I try not to lie.

LÓPEZ LECUBE: When do you lie? You don't lie to journalists.

BORGES: No, I am very naive with journalists. Everyone celebrates my humor and my irony. I have never been ironic as far as I know, I can't; irony exhausts me. If I speak insolently, everyone says "How wonderful, what lovely irony"; "What marvelous mockery." But I haven't mocked anyone.

LÓPEZ LECUBE: You said once that you have always been in love with a woman.

BORGES: Yes, but the women have changed over time.

LÓPEZ LECUBE: Have you had so many loves?

BORGES: I asked my sister about her first love and she said to me, "I don't remember much from my life but I know that I've been in love since I was four years old," and as far as I remember I have always been in love, but the people change. The love is always the same, and the person is always unique, even if she is different.

LÓPEZ LECUBE: Who is that unique person?

BORGES: There have been so many that I've lost track.

LÓPEZ LECUBE: Have you been in love with many women?

BORGES: It would be very strange if I hadn't.

LÓPEZ LECUBE: Because I would say that actually one has very few great loves.

BORGES: All love is great, love doesn't come in different sizes, whenever one is in love, they're in love with a unique person. Maybe every person is unique, maybe when one is in love they see a person as they really are, or how God sees them. If not, why fall in love with them? Maybe every person is unique, I could go further: maybe every ant is unique, if not why are there so many of them? Why else would God like ants so much? There are millions of ants and each one is undoubtedly as individual as, well, as Shakespeare or Walt Whitman. Every ant is undoubtedly unique. And every person is unique.

LÓPEZ LECUBE: Like women . . . ? The species known as woman?

BORGES: I think that they're more sensible than men, I have no doubt that if women governed countries, there would be no wars, men are irrational, they've evolved that way, women too.

LÓPEZ LECUBE: So why aren't women allowed to govern countries?

BORGES: Well, they probably have somewhere . . . I was

talking to Alicia Moreau de Justo[17] who seems a miraculous person to me; she's about to turn a hundred and she speaks so fluently. She can put together long, complex phrases and each phrase has a certain elegance. I was genuinely amazed for the first time in my life, really, a few months ago at her house, which is in Cinco Esquinas.[18] The tenement where Leónidas Barletta was born used to stand where her house is now, in Juncal and Libertad, and Barletta used to say to me "I'm a *compadrito* from Cinco Esquinas."[19] In the end he came into town. He liked to play the guitar and knew how to improvise, he was very good. Once he dedicated a song to Mastronardi that lasted maybe a quarter of an hour, all improvised, the whole thing, it came to him very easily.

LÓPEZ LECUBE: You left your mother's bedroom untouched. Why did your mother mean so much to you? Well, mothers are important to everyone, aren't they ...

BORGES: I felt that I had no right. She said to me that when she died, I should make it into my study, and that meant moving all of my books there, but I left the bed.

LÓPEZ LECUBE: To remember her by?

17 Alicia Moreau de Justo (1885–1986), Argentine politician and one of the country's first female doctors.
18 A neighborhood in Buenos Aires.
19 "Compadrito" is a *lunfardo* term for "street-kid" or "scoundrel."

BORGES: I didn't think I had the right ...

LÓPEZ LECUBE: To move it ...

BORGES: To move it, yes. Also, if I were to move it I'd almost be accentuating the difference between one era and another, but if I keep things more or less as they were ...

LÓPEZ LECUBE: It's your way of keeping her here.

BORGES: Yes, it's a way of stopping time a little, when I go back there I think that she's in her room ...

LÓPEZ LECUBE: Waiting ...

BORGES: Waiting for me, yes. About a month ago, I went to Recoleta,[20] and saw our tomb, which is horrible, like all tombs, and I thought, "Well, if there's somewhere in the world where my parents, grandparents and great-grandparents aren't, it's here." Why should I think that they're in a horrible place like Recoleta? It's odd that they've put so many restaurants in an unpleasant place like Recoleta, there's something morbid about Argentines, wanting to be close to death, don't you think?

LÓPEZ LECUBE: And where is your mother buried?

20 A wealthy neighborhood in Buenos Aires with a famous cemetery.

BORGES: In the tomb where my great-grandfather Colonel Suárez is buried with his close friend Olavarría; they both fought in the campaign in the Andes, the campaign in Brazil, they fought in the civil wars together and died together in exile, even though my great-grandfather was related to Rosas,[21] but he was proudly Unitarian.[22] They died within a few months of each other in Montevideo, which was under siege from Oribe's Blancos[23] at the time. The government gave them a pretty ugly tomb that reads "TO COLONELS SUÁREZ AND OLAVARRÍA AND THEIR DESCENDANTS," and they might bury me there, but I'd prefer, well, to be cremated, there's no ... I find the idea of being buried horrible, the corruption of the body is an awful concept.

LÓPEZ LECUBE: And facing the bars of Recoleta ...

BORGES: It's a little depressing, how odd that people decided to do that.

LÓPEZ LECUBE: So your mother asked you to make her bedroom into your study. What would you do? What will happen to your house when you die?

BORGES: It's not important. When you're dead, you're not

21 Juan Manuel de Rosas (1793–1877), Argentine dictator.
22 The Unitarian Party was a liberal political party, opposed throughout the nineteenth century by the Federal party.
23 Between 1843 and 1851, Montevideo was put under siege by the Blanco party led by General Manuel Oribe.

there. Now, what I hope is that I will be forgotten because it's all a mistake, these superficial honors, people taking me seriously all over the place. They made me a Doctor Honoris Causa in a university in Rome this year, the University of Cambridge too; I'm not seduced by those honors or by any other. I have recently been named something rather curious: I am "Rector Emeritus of the University of Caracas." What does "Rector Emeritus" mean? No one knows!

LÓPEZ LECUBE: Not even they know.

BORGES: No, they only know that it sounds good phonetically. Like Doctor Honoris Causa, what is that? And yet one gets excited. When I received my first doctorate, I got very excited. It happened in '55, '56. From the University of Cuyo.

LÓPEZ LECUBE: Was that when you went blind?

BORGES: Yes. So I travelled with my mother and we got on the train at dawn in Retiro.[24] People didn't travel by plane in those days. And we made our way across the dusty pampas, all day and all night, arriving in Mendoza a little before dawn. I was honored that same day, and I was very excited. And now I've received honors from the Sorbonne, Harvard, Oxford, Rome, Cambridge, Turin . . .

LÓPEZ LECUBE: When you're given a prize do you get the

24 Retiro is a train station and railway terminal in Buenos Aires.

same feeling you used to get when you went up on stage to get a prize at primary school?

BORGES: Well, maybe not so vivid, but you do feel something, because children are more impressed by life. My memories of childhood are very vivid.

LÓPEZ LECUBE: But do you still get excited by awards? Do they still have an effect on you?

BORGES: Yes.

LÓPEZ LECUBE: Or are you tired of prizes?

BORGES: No, no. I think *"¡Caramba! Another group of people, another group of generous, mistaken people ..."*

LÓPEZ LECUBE: Remember Borges.

BORGES: Yes, remember me.

LÓPEZ LECUBE: And yet you say you'd like to be forgotten. Why do you want to be forgotten by us? By me? I was born and you already existed ...

BORGES: Well, maybe there are already enough memories, don't you think? There's no doubt that too many books have been written, we've almost certainly got enough with just one of the different literatures, maybe too much. I taught English

literature for twenty years, at the School of Philosophy and
Letters, and I always said: "I can't teach you an infinite literature I know very little of, but I can teach you love, not for
the literature I don't know, but for some writers, no, perhaps
that's too much, some books maybe, perhaps the odd verse."
And that's plenty for me. A few months ago, a lovely thing
happened to me, one of the best experiences of my life: I was
walking down calle Maipú.

LÓPEZ LECUBE: Alone?

BORGES: No.

LÓPEZ LECUBE: With María? With María? With María, then.

BORGES: No, it wasn't María. Well, "X." I don't remember who it was, but it wasn't María. And I was stopped by a
stranger, who said to me: "I'd like to thank you for something,
Borges," and I said: "What would you like to thank me for,
sir?" And he said, "You introduced me to Robert Louis Stevenson." "Ah, well," I said to him, "in that case I feel that I
haven't lived in vain. If I've introduced you to such an admirable writer . . ." I didn't ask him who he was, because it's perfect
like that. Whoever he was, that was enough. Knowing who he
was would be redundant, useless, I was already congratulating
myself without knowing who the boy I taught around 1960
and introduced to Stevenson's work was. I thought: "Well,
now, after that, I am justified." The books I've written don't
matter. They're the least important thing.

LÓPEZ LECUBE: But why do you say that you'd like us to forget you?

BORGES: Because it's unimportant.

LÓPEZ LECUBE: What's a typical day for you?

BORGES: Well, when I'm lucky, I'm talking to you here, but I don't get lucky every day.

LÓPEZ LECUBE: Well, thank you. You don't have to say that.

BORGES: Well, I sleep a siesta.

LÓPEZ LECUBE: How many hours?

BORGES: No, for me a long siesta is forty minutes, because I take a long time to get to sleep. I find it very difficult; sometimes I even have to take a pill.

LÓPEZ LECUBE: Do you have insomnia?

BORGES: Yes, insomnia visits me quite often. There's a lovely verse by Rosetti: "Sleepless, with cold commemorative eyes ..."

LÓPEZ LECUBE: And what do you do when you have insomnia?

BORGES: I try not to think about getting to sleep. I try to think up a plot or polish a verse.

LÓPEZ LECUBE: Do you remember what you thought about the next day?

BORGES: No, but I managed to get to sleep, which is the important thing. No, happily I don't remember the projects of my insomnia. But I am always writing verses or prose, I'm always polishing verses or putting together plots for stories because if I didn't, I'd get very bored. Xul Solar[25] once said to me that he wouldn't mind spending a year in prison. "In the company of your cellmates?" "No," he said, "a year in a cell on my own." "Ah well, me too, because spending a year with criminals sounds horrible." I don't think it would be so bad, a blind person is alone; blindness is a form of solitude . . . old age too.

LÓPEZ LECUBE: What time do you get up in the morning?

BORGES: They come to wake me at nine but I'm already awake, and I try to get to sleep when I hear the Torre de los Ingleses[26] strike eleven. But sometimes I don't, sometimes I come home late and it strikes twelve and I'm disoriented. Generally I go to bed at eleven.

LÓPEZ LECUBE: And the cat?

25 Xul Solar (1887–1963), Argentine artist.
26 A clock tower in Retiro, Buenos Aires. It was a gift to Argentina from the British government to celebrate the nation's centenary.

BORGES: The cat died.

LÓPEZ LECUBE: The cat died? When did it die?

BORGES: About a month ago, I think. I think it was twelve and that's old for a cat. I didn't know it, but apparently that's a good life for a cat.

LÓPEZ LECUBE: And do you miss it?

BORGES: Yes, sometimes, and sometimes not. I look for it and then remember that it's died.

LÓPEZ LECUBE: So I should get you a little cat?

BORGES: I don't know. I'd have to ask because cats can be a lot of work and as they die, it can be hard can't it? And you'd look at it as though it were the previous cat but it would be a little different, as though it were dressed up, so I'd have to ask, but thank you very much in any case.

LÓPEZ LECUBE: All the popularity you've earned over the years.

BORGES: It's strange isn't it? But it will pass.

LÓPEZ LECUBE: Why should it pass if it's growing all the time? How does it feel? When I walk down the street with you, it causes more fuss than with Miguel Angél Solá!

BORGES: Who's Miguel Ángel Solá? Now, Émile Zola, I know that name . . .

LÓPEZ LECUBE: Miguel Ángel Solá is an actor . . . With you people stand back, amazed, it's an expression of . . .

BORGES: Well, if I were with Émile Zola that would be because he's dead; it would be an amazing sight. Walking with Émile Zola!

LÓPEZ LECUBE: And you're growing ever more popular, your wit, your genius . . .

BORGES: What can I do? And yet I'm still published, which should put people off shouldn't it? This year, I'm directing a collection of one hundred books, I wanted to call it the Marco Polo Library, but the publisher chose a more vague title, Personal Library, so that's what it's called. I'm choosing them with María Kodama, and writing the prologues.

LÓPEZ LECUBE: A good thing is happening that I want to tell you about: children are learning about you because of the advertisement on television. When I told my daughter that I was going to interview Jorge Luis Borges, she said to me: "The man who's writing all the books?"

BORGES: Well, I'm not writing them, they're books by great writers; a Personal Library.

LÓPEZ LECUBE: No, I know, but it means young people already know about you.

BORGES: Well, Bioy told me a story today; he was with a Spanish woman at his home, and a package of books arrived from the printers: fifty copies. She looked at it and he said, "Yes, I wrote them." So she opened the package and saw that they were fifty copies of the same book and said to him "There's been a mistake! They're all the same!" She was very disappointed; she was expecting fifty different books! As they were all the same, she must have said to herself "*Caramba,* this man's an impostor! *Caramba,* what a poseur!" "Yes," he said to me, "I reproached myself; just one book!" [*Laughing.*] It would seem that she knew nothing about editions, of course. And especially that she was unfamiliar with the concept of fifty first editions.

LÓPEZ LECUBE: Do you live on a pension?

BORGES: Yes, I have two pensions: I was the director of the National Library, and I resigned when I heard that he had come back to power. Well, we know the story don't we? He was called . . .

LÓPEZ LECUBE: Say it! Say it!

BORGES: What they call Cangallo now.[27] That's it, the man who's now known as Cangallo. I left because I couldn't in good conscience serve him, it would be ridiculous. And then I was an English literature professor and I let go of my anger, and I have two pensions. Books don't make enough to live on in this country; a friend of mine sadly resigned himself to writing pornography, he tried to live off the dirty words he learned in third grade, to writing about the sexual act, and he was very melancholy. Then it turned out that even these universal studies weren't enough to make him prosperous and he's still poor. Because pornography isn't enough, obscenity isn't enough to maintain oneself. Apparently not. And that means that nothing will be enough.

LÓPEZ LECUBE: No?

BORGES: Well, it seems that nothing is enough; everything is so difficult these days.

LÓPEZ LECUBE: Borges, you say that you don't read the newspapers and yet you know about everything that goes on in politics because you offer opinions on everything.

27 Borges is referring to the former Argentine president Juan Domingo Perón (1895–1974), whose government he fiercely opposed in the 1940s and '50s. In 1973, Perón returned from exile in Spain, to take control of the government once more and Borges resigned his post at the National Library. Cangallo is a major street in Buenos Aires that was renamed Juan Domingo Perón and then changed back after his government fell.

BORGES: Well, my friends keep me informed, but I have never read a newspaper in my life. I realized that something that lasts a day can't be very important, can it? They call them dailies, which doesn't inspire much confidence, does it?

LÓPEZ LECUBE: Before, you didn't get involved in politics . . .

BORGES: And I still don't, I don't belong to any party.

LÓPEZ LECUBE: And yet your opinions can be harsh . . .

BORGES: Yes, but for ethical reasons, not political ones. When I was young I started out as a Communist, around 1918, committed to universal brotherhood, the absence of borders, friendship between all men. And then, who knows why, I became a Radical, I was a Conservative, and now I don't belong to any party.

LÓPEZ LECUBE: But never a Peronist.

BORGES: Well, I like to think that I'm a gentleman, a decent person.

LÓPEZ LECUBE: So you're still a committed anti-Peronist. I thought from some of the statements you've made that you'd forgiven a little.

BORGES: Forgotten, not forgiven. Forgetting is the only form of forgiveness, it's the only vengeance and the only punishment too. Because if my counterpart sees that I'm still thinking about them, in some ways I become their slave, and if I forget them I don't. I think that forgiveness and vengeance are two words for the same substance, which is oblivion. But one does not forget a wrong easily.

LÓPEZ LECUBE: And have you forgotten?

BORGES: Well, I think of my mother, who was in prison for a month, my sister too, apart from what happened to me. They were imprisoned for a month and a day and if I don't think about that, I think about how they've debased the country as well as ransacking it.

LÓPEZ LECUBE: Do you know that there are writers who charge for interviews? You're someone . . .

BORGES: Well, I really have no idea how much you're going to pay me.

LÓPEZ LECUBE: [*Laughing.*] We can talk about that later.

BORGES: I think nothing, don't you? Let's set it at zero then, is zero fine with you?

LÓPEZ LECUBE: Of course, zero. Silvia Bullrich[28] charges in dollars.

28 Silvia Bullrich (1915–1990), Argentine writer.

BORGES: Well, Silvia Bullrich is a rich woman and I'm a poor man. It's strange that rich people are usually miserly and often greedy too. Poor people aren't, the poor are free with their generosity. Poor people are generous, rich people aren't. My father used to say to me that when one inherits a fortune, they inherit the conditions that led to making that fortune, meaning that rich people inherit wealth and the qualities of miserliness and greed, which it maybe requires.

LÓPEZ LECUBE: That's wonderful, you mean that one can't be rich without stealing from someone?

BORGES: I think so, property is originally a theft.

LÓPEZ LECUBE: Property is theft?

BORGES: The problem is that you and I aren't Guaraní Indians or Charrua Indians, we have no right to be here, of course.

LÓPEZ LECUBE: Working hard . . .

BORGES: Working hard . . .

LÓPEZ LECUBE: And at zero, as you just said.

BORGES: Many thanks.

JORGE LUIS BORGES (1899–1986) was an Argentine author, essayist, poet, translator, lecturer, and librarian who gained worldwide recognition after receiving, in 1961, the first International Publishers Prize, which he shared with Samuel Beckett. Borges wrote innovative fiction combining the fantastic and the metaphysical, and is best known for the short-story collections *Ficciones* (1944) and *The Aleph* (1949). He died in Geneva in 1986.

RICHARD BURGIN, the editor of the literary magazine *Boulevard* and the winner of five Pushcart Prizes for his stories, is the author of sixteen books, including two novels, nine collections of stories, and two books of nonfiction, *Conversations with Isaac Bashevis Singer* and *Conversations with Jorge Luis Borges*.

DANIEL BOURNE has edited *Artful Dodge* since its inception in 1979. His books of poetry include *The Household Gods* and *Where No One Spoke the Language*. He teaches English at the College of Wooster.

STEPHEN CAPE (1953–2010) was a longtime cataloger of rare books at the Lilly Library at Indiana University. He was also the poetry editor for *Artful Dodge* during the early 1980s.

CHARLES SILVER is a visual artist and former editor of *Artful Dodge*.

GLORIA LÓPEZ LECUBE was born in Buenos Aires. She has worked as a journalist in print, radio, and television, and also managed two radio stations. She interviewed Borges in 1985, just before he left Argentina for Geneva.

KIT MAUDE is a Buenos Aires–based translator and editor.

THE LAST INTERVIEW SERIES

KURT VONNEGUT: THE LAST INTERVIEW

"I think it can be tremendously refreshing if a creator of literature has something on his mind other than the history of literature so far. Literature should not disappear up its own asshole, so to speak."

$15.95 / $17.95 CAN
978-1-61219-090-7
ebook: 978-1-61219-091-4

LEARNING TO LIVE FINALLY: THE LAST INTERVIEW
JACQUES DERRIDA

"I am at war with myself, it's true, you couldn't possibly know to what extent . . . I say contradictory things that are, we might say, in real tension; they are what construct me, make me live, and will make me die."

translated by PASCAL-ANNE BRAULT and MICHAEL NAAS

$15.95 / $17.95 CAN
978-1-61219-094-5
ebook: 978-1-61219-032-7

ROBERTO BOLAÑO: THE LAST INTERVIEW

"Posthumous: It sounds like the name of a Roman gladiator, an unconquered gladiator. At least that's what poor Posthumous would like to believe. It gives him courage."

translated by SYBIL PEREZ and others

$15.95 / $17.95 CAN
978-1-61219-095-2
ebook: 978-1-61219-033-4

THE LAST INTERVIEW SERIES

DAVID FOSTER WALLACE: THE LAST INTERVIEW

"I don't know what you're thinking or what it's like inside you and you don't know what it's like inside me. In fiction... we can leap over that wall itself in a certain way."

$15.95 / $15.95 CAN
978-1-61219-206-2
ebook: 978-1-61219-207-9

JORGE LUIS BORGES: THE LAST INTERVIEW

"Believe me: the benefits of blindness have been greatly exaggerated. If I could see, I would never leave the house, I'd stay indoors reading the many books that surround me."

translated by KIT MAUDE

$15.95 / $15.95 CAN
978-1-61219-204-8
ebook: 978-1-61219-205-5